Essayistic Ventures
and
Topical Asides

Essayistic Ventures

AND

Topical Asides

By

Joseph Mileck

Pensive Oasis
Berkeley, California
2017

ISBN (paperback): 978-0-9982685-2-1
ISBN (ebook): 978-0-9982685-3-8

Printed in the United States of America

Design and Layout: Rick Soldin (book-comp.com)

Pensive Oasis, Berkeley, California

Thought begets Thought

Contents

Essayistic Ventures and Topical Asides

Preamble

The Essay's Origin

The essay, one of the Western World's most popular genres of literature, has had a very checkered history. It had its origins in Greek and Roman antiquity (Theophrastus, 371–288 B.C., Plutarch, A.D. 46–120; Cicero, 106–41 B.C., Seneca, 4 B.C.–A.D. 65), spread nameless through Europe during the Middle Ages and the Renaissance, and did not acquire its name until Michel de Montaigne (1533–1592), father of the French essay, published short experimental prose ventures in a book entitled *Essais* (1580).

Reader enthusiasm and writer interest in Montaigne's new experimental pieces were immediate in France and spread quickly to England, where Francis Bacon (1561–1626), influenced by Montaigne, and like Montaigne, very mindful of classical antiquity, published some fifty-six essays between 1599 and 1625.

Montaigne's very personal, off-the-cuff, ironic and provocative "essais", and Bacon's tight-lipped, disciplined and instructive "essayes" became the springboard of the Western World's widespread, very variegated, and still evolving essay.

The British Essay

Reader interest in Bacon's sober essayistic analysis of the self and of society was immediate and spread rapidly and Bacon's essays, like Montaigne's, also quickly attracted the attention of England's younger writers. By the end of the 17th century—thanks to such writers as Thomas Browne (1605–1682), Abraham Cowley (1618–1667),

John Dryden (1631–1700), Owen Feltham (1602–1668), James Howell (1594–1666) and Ben Jonson (1574–1637)—the English essay had found its place among the literature's older genres.

The English essay budded in the 17th century, then burst into extravagant bloom in the course of the 18th. The genre's brevity and sobriety appealed immediately, its didactic and entertainment propensity attracted, and its ready availability in a scattering of popular newspapers (e.g. *The Champion Bee, Free Thinker, Plain Dealer, Rambler, Spectator*, and *The Tatler*) and significant periodicals (e.g. *Monthly Review, Critical Review*) served its purpose. For England's growing body of middle-class readers, essays of every ilk became serial reading.

This veritable vogue of the 18th century enriched English literature as no other genre. Thanks to England's 18th century, students of English literature commonly look upon the essay as something peculiarly English, and as one of the glories of English letters.

It was not blind chance that propelled the English essay from insignificance to prominence. General and specific circumstances were propitious. The English essay could not have had more ideal models than Montaigne and Bacon, England's middle class was amply receptive, the press was only too eager to print, and some of the best of England's literary minds quickly committed themselves to the new genre (among them: Joseph Addison, 1672–1719, Richard Cumberland, 1732–1811, Henry Fielding, 1707–1754, Oliver Goldsmith, 1728–1774, Samuel Johnson, 1709–1784, Alexander Pope, 1688–1744, Richard Steele, 1672–1729, and Jonathan Swift, 1667–1745).

By the end of the 18th century, England's preoccupation with the essay had begun to wane and new literary interests to surface. Readers and writers drifted from personal down-to-earth essay to the other-worldly sentimental poetry of the romantic era and then to the serious socially conscious novels of the industrialized Victorian Age—a literary consequence of England's cultural drift.

However, despite this general 19th century growing disinterest in the essay, enough of England's letter writers (among them: Matthew Arnold, 1822–1884, Thomas Carlyle, 1795–1881, William Hazlitt,

1778–1830, Charles Lamb, 1775–1834, Thomas Macaulay, 1800–1850, John Ruskin, 1819–1900, John Henry Newman, 1801–1890, R.L. Stevenson, 1850–1894) did remain enough taken with the genre to keep it from becoming something of but a spent literary curiosity.

Though England's literary world has, generally and to date, fared right well, its essay has continued its 19th century progressive decline. A genre once favored by England's best writers and avid middle-class readers began to find ever fewer of both, and for good reason. Modern England's ever more harried middle class began to find ever less time for such cultural matters as writing and reading, distracted as it became ever more by the Modern World's plethora of time-consuming seductive novelties (telephone, radio, movies, videos, television, internet, computer and the Electronics Age's myriad devices and apps), by an entertaining ever burgeoning world of sport, and by the ease and comfort of pleasure travel.

Cultural distractions left the 20th century essayist or would-be essay writer with less time for writing, and the reader with less time for reading. The reading public's resultant growing disinterest in the essay reduced the essayist's interest in writing essays. And the considerable writing skills that the essay demanded persuaded many essayists and would-be essayists to opt for such more popular and less challenging forms of writing as newspaper columns, newspaper reports, commentaries, talks and casual articles.

Though popularly in progressive decline in the 20th century, the British essay continued to attract the attention of a fair number of England's better writers, among them: Max Beerbohm (1872–1956), Hilaire Belloc (1870–1953), G.K. Chesterton (1874–1936), Joseph Conrad (1867–1924), James Joyce (1852–1941), Arthur Koestler (1905–1983), D.H. Lawrence (1885–1930), K. Ogden (1880–1947), Rose Macaulay (1891–1958), George Orwell (1903–1950), Dorothy Richardson (1873–1957), John Wain (1925–1994), and H.G. Wells (1866–1946).

This continued writing of exemplary essays by these noteworthies and particularly John Berger's (1926–2017) some five book collections of his colorful and provocative essays of the turn of the century (among them: *Photocopies: Encounters,* Pantheon, 1998, 180 pp.; *Selected Essays,* Penguin, 2003, 608 pp.; *Confabulations*, Penguin, 2016, 160 pp.) suggests that a revival of the English essay may be in the offing. Time will tell!

Characterization and Definition of the Essay

*T*he essayist has been something of a literary up-start, a maverick among writers, a free spirit little mindful of the matter and manner strictures of a literary genre. He has gone his way and done his thing, toying with the substance, form, intent and tone of his art, and leaving in his wake a plethora of variegated examples of a new literary genre: the essay.

It all began with Montaigne's characteristically spontaneous whimsical and provocative "essais" focussed on self and life, and with Bacon's typically disciplined aphoristic "essayes" broadly preoccupied with the human condition. Under the influence of both Montaigne and Bacon, a new genre of literature emerged: the English essay. The new form of literature spread rapidly, never stopped evolving freely ad capriciously, and in time became a genre that, in its variableness, challenges memorable characterization.

What is the British essay but an art form that dwells briefly, and in a very personal and discursive or cool and collected manner, on some person, thing, place, incident, event or on whatever interest that may be personal or of general interest. The genre is generally of some four or five pages, is often many more pages in length, and is rarely even but a single paragraph. It is of the prose family, but does also flirt with poetry. The essay's widely ranging matter, either bland or learned, is treated quite formally or very informally, is intent upon informing, instructing, persuading or simply upon entertaining, and the tone of the essay's message can range from the jocular to the trenchant.

Genre characterizations, such as the above, though right telling, are generally and quickly forgotten. Students of literature might do well to turn from quickly forgotten general characterization to more

Essayistic Ventures and Topical Asides

memorable and more quotable silhouetted definition, such as: The essay is a brief personal expression of private opinion intent upon informing and instructing.

The American Essay

*T*he essay found its way to England at a culturally most propitious time. Bacon's essays immediately attracted an ever-growing number of middle-class readers and young writers; by the end of the 17th century, the English essay was a genre of choice; and by the middle of the 18th century, the English essay was considered the most English of all literary genres.

Such was not the early lot of the American essay. Colonial America was sparsely populated, was of necessity more given to mundane matters than to the literary world, and resultantly had but relatively few writers and readers. Until the 19th century, while the English essay was flourishing, the American essay little more than just survived. The essays written by such of America's few pre-19th century writers as Anne Bradstreet (1612–1672), Mary Rowlandson (1637–1711) and Jonathan Edwards (1703–1758), are as distinctly American as Bacon's are British.

As expected, these early American essays dwell almost exclusively upon the ordeals of life in the New World and upon Indian affairs, and are imbued with Puritanical religiosity. In their manner and tone, these essays differ no less drastically from their contemporary British counterparts than in their matter. The Colonial essay characteristically ranges more freely in its length than the British essay, is also more loosely structured, and its language is less sophisticated. The Colonial essay is also typically more narrative and less discursive than its English counterpart. And since many of America's early-day essayists were ministers, it is little wonder that many Colonial essays are more sermons than essays.

Such was the general lot of the American essay until the 19th century, but for an unexpected brief flurry of very-well written and highly informed philosophical and political essays written by such revolutionary worthies as John Adams (1735–1826), Samuel Adams (1722–1803), Benjamin Franklin (1706–1790), Alexander Hamilton (1755–1804), John Jay (1745–1820), Thomas Jefferson (1743–1826), James Madison (1751–1836) and Thomas Paine (1737–1809).

It was not until the 19th century that the American essay came into its own, thanks to such of America's best thinkers and writers as Emily Dickinson (1810–1886), Ralph Waldo Emerson (1803–1882), Washington Irving (1783–1859), James Russell Lowell (1819–1891), Herman Melville (1819–1891), Edgar Allen Poe (1803–1849), Henry David Thoreau (1817–1862), Mark Twain (1835–1910), Oliver Wendell Holmes (1809–1894) and Walt Whitman (1819–1892). The American essay was finally on a par with the British in both matter and manner. A provincial Colonial essay was now a widely-read, very sophisticated literary genre that informed, edified and inspired.

In matter, the reach of the new essay extended from philosophy, religion, politics and war to the arts and aesthetics, to the universe, nature and weather, and to such simple pastimes as walking and fishing. Little was now beyond erudite essayistic opinion. Cosmopolitanized matter found its appropriate transfigured manner.

In its manner, the 19th century essay became less immediate and friendly, and more removed and formal than the Colonial essay. Awkward language gave way to sophisticated polished prose, and highly intellectual discussion supplanted the simple narration of the Colonial years.

Though veritably transfigured in its evolution from the 17th to the 19th century, the American essay had remained within the parameters of its genre. This was not to be the case in the essay's further evolution in the 20th century and beyond.

The horizon of literary possibility in America began to recede before the First World War, and this recession has continued progressively to the present. America of the 20th and 21st centuries has been an ever more erratically changing world. America's stream of wars from the First World War to its military involvements in the Middle East and

Essayistic Ventures and Topical Asides

beyond, its depression of the 20th and that of the 21st century, its Cold War with Russia, its imperial aspirations, its financial, political and religious divides, its Electronics Age, its wanting schools and medical care and its national political gridlock have left the nation in social, political and cultural turmoil. Political and social upheaval have had a devastating impact upon the general welfare of America, while cultural turmoil spawned an exciting rush of literary experimentation. The innovative creativity of such dramatist as Eugene O'Neill, Tennessee Williams and Thornton Wilder, such poets as Robert Frost, Carl Sandberg and Vachel LIndsay, and such novelists as Ernest Hemingway, W.H. Faulkner and John Steinbeck virtually illuminated America's literary world. On the other hand, America's modernist essayists, in their experimental fervor, began gradually to disregard all standard strictures of matter and manner, eventually leaving their genre decimated.

Given cultural fatigue, changing interests and the attraction of novelty and experiment, it was inevitable that America's sophisticated demanding 19th century essay would not remain intact. By the middle of the 20th century, it was obvious that America's erudite opinion piece was a thing of the past, a new free-wheeling literary pastime.

Modernist American essayists began to disregard the genre's traditional strictures of matter and manner, and to fashion their own ever more idiosyncratic opinion pieces. In length, essays began to range from a simple paragraph to fifty pages and more, and hybrid poetry-prose and epistolary essays became common. The polished mode of expression characteristic of the 19th century essay gradually gave way to a more informal every-day or peculiarly radicalized language. Matter began to range no less freely than manner. Interest ranged from the very serious to the trivial, from autobiography, recollection, rumination, racism, gender issues, disarmament, national and global politics and world peace, to boxing, customized cars and common gossip. But few subjects were more or less off limits, and most of everything was humorized, fantasized or satirized.

These modernist essays, written in the first three quarters of the 20th century, represent the twilight of America's traditional essay.

Their many writers—such as James Baldwin (1923–1987), John Cage (1912–1992), W.E.B. DuBois (1868–1963), T.S. Eliot (1888–1965), F. Scott Fitzgerald (1896–1940), William Gars (1924–), Norman Mailer (1923–2007), Ch. Morley (1890–1957), Agnes Rapplier (1858–1950), Gertrude Stein (1874–1946), William Carlos Williams (1888–1963), Tom Wolfe (1900–1938)—are the last of America's preeminent essayists. America's so-called essayists of the past fifty years are not to be identified with its modernist twilight essayists. These writers, among them D. Barthelme (1931–1987), Jenny Boully (1936–), Anne Carson (1950–), Joan Didion (1934–), Annie Dillard (1945–), Harry Mathews (1930–2017), John McPhee (1931–), Caille Milner (1979–), Susan Mitchell (1944–), N.S. Momaday (1934–), Susan Sontag (1933–2004), Gay Talese (1932–), David Wallace (1962–2008) and Eliot Weinberger (1949–), are essentially not essayists but, by and large, a vanguard breed of eccentric writers given almost capriciously to new literary possibility. Their trail of solipsistic literary novelties knows no strictures of matter or manner. These are brash free spirits, whose odd ventures are clearly art for the artist's sake and not for the reader's sake.

In matter, these current faux or unconventional essays are characteristically something about anything from bland travelogue to cryptic lectures, politics to finances, meaningless enumeration of stray facts to simple letters, medical care to education, boring fantasies to vague ruminations, religion to terrorism, casual notes and directions to recipes, peace and war to philosophy, and from pointless chatter to obscure snatches of diary.

This highly variable subject matter finds its highly variable modes of expression. One faux essay may consist of but a one-line sentence, another of but one short paragraph, another of but one sentence six pages in length, and another of more than fifty pages, and yet another may be but a segment of a book. Some faux essays are but poems, some very short and others quite protracted, some are akin to one-act dramas, and still others are snatches of absurd prose. The language of these faux essays ranges from everyday chatter to flowery literary prose, and from the formal mode of expression of scholars

Essayistic Ventures and Topical Asides

to the reportage of newspapers. And almost all matter is commonly slightly fantasized, humorized or satirized.

The writers of these many faux essays are not true essayists, and their works are clearly not true essays. These unorthodox writers are not the astute observers of self and life intent upon informing and instructing their readers that America's bona fide essayists were, but aspiring self-centered writers intent upon playing experimentally with the possibilities of their craft, and intent upon toying with, amusing, teasing and baffling their readers.

How much longer this period of literary experimentation will continue to flourish, and when America's true essay will awaken from its present slumber, as surely it eventually will, is a guess at best. Many faux essayists have already given up experiment to become newspaper reporters and columnists, radio and television commentators, and fiction and article writers, and a fair number has also opted to shift its attention to the old essay. If this growing number of essay converts should manage to attract a new generation of young essayists, and if such impressive collections of essays as those edited and introduced by John D'Agata (*The Next American Essay*, 2003, 475 pp., *The Lost Origins of the Essay*, 2016, 689 pp., *The Making of the American Essay*, 2016, 798 pp., all published by Graywolf Press, Minneapolis, Minnesota), should manage to restore popular interest in the essay, a revival of the genre may soon be in the offing. We shall see!

Joseph Mileck

Foreword

*T*he trail of chronically arranged Essayistic Ventures and Topical Asides began in the middle seventies of the past century and ended in 2016. These forty years of close observation and serious reflection started with a slow accumulation of pastime ruminations that quickly became a deliberate intellectual diary of essays and casual asides that record their author's flow of interests and evolving thought, and mirror a society's social and cultural course.

These essayistic ventures, like the traditional American essay, are uninhibited in their range of interests. The general *condition humaine*, life and death and peace and war, attracts its fair share of attention, as does the political world, democracy, autocracy and imperialism. Matters philosophical, psychological, religious, scientific and economic provide plentiful fodder for discussion, and America's cultural/social world—its government and sundry institutions, its medical care, education and prisons, and its age of electronics—is ready matter for chronic studied comment. And current events of general significance and personal interest, and a few public dignitaries and notorieties have their merited share of attention.

These essayistic ventures and asides emulate the manner of the traditional essay no less than they do its matter. Their variable brevity, studied structure and formal language are reminiscent of the composition of the old essay. And like the traditional essay, these current efforts are intent upon information, instruction and improvement.

It is hoped that this return to the traditional American essay resonates positively with readers and writers, and so much as to persuade a fair number of these to attempt their own essays. Such could help to energize a pending popular revival of the venerable essay.

March 2017

A TRAIL
OF
ESSAYISTIC VENTURES

Oh yes, dear reader, the essay is alive.

There is no reason to despair.

(Virginia Woolf)

Cultural Decline

A culture, at its best, nurtures and strives to live in accordance with its social, political, economic, philosophical, moral and religious myths.
A culture in decline, mouths but does not live its myths.
A culture spent, just wallows wildly in the debris of its dead myths.
Our western culture is writhing obliviously in the throes of its disintegration!
It all recalls the final frenzied days of Rome and of Athens, and like these past cultures, it also presages a future culture.
Cultures, like flowers, grow and glow, then shrivel and blow!
Nor does the individual escape this change and flow!

The Jews of America

*A*t the beginning of the 20th century, Jews in America were insularized willingly, of necessity and forcibly. They clung to their racial origin, their religious roots and to their East European cultural background. Together, these were their identity. Jewish life ran its course in the ghetto, revolved around the synagogue and the yeshivas, and Yiddish was its language.

The more than two million Jews who immigrated from the eighties of the 19th century to the twenties of the 20th century were separated from the mainstream of American life both internally and externally. This was no less true of the Polish, Irish, Italian, German, Dutch, Swedish and sundry other immigrants. Virtually all immigrant minorities had this common beginning. Integration followed, more slowly for some minorities and more rapidly for others, complete integration for most and only partial integration for some. Poles, Germans, Italians *et al.* first became Polish-Americans, German-Americans, Italian-Americans, and then, after three generations at most, simply Americans, and with this, assimilation was more or less complete.

Jewish absorption has been an exception! It has not really proceeded beyond the intermediate hyphenated identity. Jews, though culturally, economically and politically integrated, have clung tenaciously to their Jewish racial-religious identity, to their basic difference. Most people born in the U.S.A. consider themselves to be Americans who chance to have European or other ancestors while many or most Jews born in the U.S.A. consider themselves Jews who have by chance been born in America. Many or most Jews thus have a double identity: they are Jews and Americans. And thereby, the Jews have managed, wonder of wonders, to achieve the virtually impossible: retention of original identity and integration.

Jews have had, unfortunately, to pay a price for their straddling, and they continue to pay that price: anti-Semitism. The native many never have, and likely never will fully embrace the different, the stranger, the minority intent upon nurturing and retaining its difference.

Cultural Death

Deconstruction is the passion of our times,
The final consequence of Einstein's theory of relativity.
Vanguard intellectuals in every field are tearing asunder in self-promotional frenzy,
And the masses are indifferent, or somewhat puzzled, or wallowing in the resultant new-born liberties.
Cultures and civilizations once died a slow natural death, as their core beliefs and values fell by the wayside.
The warp and woof of the thread-bare carpet of our Judeo-Christian Western World are, in contrast, being torn apart in relative frenzy.
Our cultural death is simply too slow for thinking vultures.
Deconstructionists will of course die with their prey,
New constructionists will then have their way and a new culture will have its day.

In Memoriam

The Idiosyncrasies of a Lovable Eccentric
Dr. Gerald Hirschberg (1914–2004)

*P*rofessionally, Jerry was an exceptionally dedicated and competent physician, and personally, he was both a startling and amusing eccentric. Jerry's patients can attest to his professional skill and care; I, a friend of more than fifty years, would like to dwell briefly on just a few of his eccentricities.

Jerry was a tenacious sleuth in the field of physical medicine and he rose admirably to the challenges of the world. He was also decidedly at home in the intellectual world and proved to be a veritable Jesuit in argument. But in the complex emotional interplay of humans, he was, figuratively speaking, tone deaf, a baffled novice. Needless to say, psychology and all related specialties held little appeal for him and did anything but enjoy his respect. It was in this daunting minefield of interpersonal relationships that Jerry had to learn to cope professionally and personally. Jerry did both successfully and in his own peculiar ways.

Basically shy and fearful, plagued by low self-esteem, insecurities and phobias, and hypersensitive to slight, Jerry managed notwithstanding to adapt resourcefully and to advantage: in protective reaction, he became an argumentatively able loner, and to claim his place in the sun, an excellent though a somewhat arrogant doctor.

Awkward outsider though he was, Jerry always managed to find the few colleagues and friends professionally and socially necessary in his withdrawn adjustment to life. This resourceful tactic began in France, became progressively more successful in New York, then Virginia, and was perfected in California. Inept as Jerry was in medical politics and gauche in social relationships, he literally needed these colleagues and friends to run interference for him to further his career and to provide him with the modicum of social content he desired and needed. These mentors were no fools. In Jerry, they saw an ambitious and innovative doctor and a decent human being, both in need of their help. Enduring relationships evolved and both parties benefited.

Joseph Mileck

While Jerry's model-mentors managed ably to accommodate the basic needs of Jerry the loner, Jerry took it upon himself to dispose of life's lesser challenges, and again in his own resourceful idiosyncratic manner. Contrary to his own convictions, Jerry was never more than just a fair car driver. On the other hand, he was almost paranoidally safety-minded; he always preferred to drive clearly visible tank-like Suburbans, rarely exceeded speed limits, carefully kept more than ample distance between himself and the road's center stripe and never attempted to park on crowded city streets. These precautionary measures did prevent major collisions and did assure Jerry's own safety, his major concern, but over the years also left a trail of shattered side-view mirrors to the right of Jerry's lumbering SUV and not a few rear-ended and side swiped cars at Andronico's, Jerry's favorite parking lot. Surprisingly enough, these many mishaps were simply too minor for Jerry to brake or to report to the police. No one was ever hurt and that was good enough!

Far more amusing than Jerry's response or lack of response to broken mirrors and dented cars was his recourse to an ingenious driving tactic to counter his rapidly diminishing skills following his 75th birthday. Stiff of waist, disinclined for pain to turn his head either to the right or to the left and progressively slower in his driving reactions, Jerry concluded after much ratiocination that all left turns, except those at stoplights, had become too hazardous for him. Straight ahead and to the right now began to characterize Jerry's defensive maneuvers. His daily safari for provisions at Andronico's and coffee at Starbucks now became a very circuitous journey. With but an exceptionally necessary dangerous left turn, Jerry always managed to get there and back home without any major collisions. Needless to say, Jerry the eccentric was very proud of his idiosyncratic solution to a vexing problem. Wife Susi, on the other hand, only scoffed and continued her customary loud and biting backseat verbal navigation. In opinion, just as in most things controversial, ne'er the twain did meet.

Jerry clearly marched to his own drummer and, more often than not, that drummer struck a consistently idiosyncratic beat. For Jerry, and no less for Susi, decisions were difficult, changes distressing and action always tardy and tentative. A well-worn living room rug with an ever larger-growing hole was not replaced but at long last only refaced by placing a stray piece of carpet over the offending gap. A jagged hole in a rotting deck, faring no better, was simply hidden under a piece of plywood and then not until it had become a hazard for both man and beast. To conceal was obviously less demanding of thought and effort than to repair or have repaired, and this for Jerry had become a standard practice.

Jerry had better things to do in life than to tend to menial matters of repair. He had become something of an amateur botanist. He knew his wildflowers by their Latin appellations and he delighted in commenting on their petals, stamens and pistils, but, alas, he had no green thumb. Convinced, nevertheless, that he could emulate nature, Jerry began enthusiastically to scatter wildflower seeds over his uncultivated and disheveled hillside, and it seemed as though he would continue to do so forever even though no flower ever emerged to adorn his hill. It was almost a decade before Jerry finally desisted but not until one of his more down-to-earth friends managed to convince him that his soil was too poor, too dry and too hard, and that the neighborhood's many birds were too opportunistic to expect any success. This stubbornly pursued annual ritual was probably one of the most irrational of Jerry's more than just a few futile idiosyncratic ventures. A smattering of common sense could have saved Jerry considerable time, effort and expense, but then as Jerry would argue, common sense was of and for the common many and he was no common person.

Jerry loved to eat and he ate bountifully. He fancied himself something of an expert in French cuisine and was particularly partial to bouillabaisse. Since elegant restaurants and formal attire were not Jerry's cup of tea, he never found the bouillabaisse so eagerly sought and many a simple cook was less than politely taken to task for Americanizing this favorite dish. Jerry did not give up this practice until one of his closer friends simply refused to continue to dine out with him.

Jerry's bedside manner could be almost as assaulting as his untoward disposal of would-be chefs. His customarily demanded verbally unelaborated yes or no in response to his medical questions left the timid among his patients thoroughly intimidated. Jerry remained oblivious of this impact until one of his psychologically astute colleagues drew it to his attention and then persuaded him to have recourse to a gentler tactic.

These embarrassing interactions always seemed completely out of keeping with a sensitive temperament fearful of any confrontation. Hindsight suggests that this apparently anomalous behavior was but another idiosyncratic expression of Jerry's naïve candor. He was characteristically more or less oblivious of the impact of his gruff frankness on others. When taken to task for his bluntness, though puzzled, he would quickly become abjectly apologetic. Much more in keeping with Jerry's passive being was his frantic flight down the street, after a marital misstep, with Susi, knife in hand, in hot pursuit and loud in invective.

Jerry could be just as naively assuaging as he could be brusquely insulting. He and I and his dog often took to the track and to running. The longer we ran the more spirited leashless Daisy would become and the more fellow runners she would jump. In the bedlam of angry shouts and fearful screams that often followed, Jerry was always surprisingly calm as he quietly tried to persuade the victims that Daisy's assaults were only playful expressions of love. The return doubtful glances always left Jerry perplexed. He simply could not put himself into their shoes, another of his many idiosyncratic actions and reactions.

For Jerry, just as for victims of Asperger's Syndrome, the human scene was exceedingly perplexing. Humans were more or less beyond his fathoming and he beyond their appreciation. His response was to go his own way and to do his own thing and to have as little truck with others as necessary and salutary. He structured his life accordingly: regularly to bed by eight and up by five and in between primarily medically preoccupied. There was little interest in, or time for socializing or for hobbies. Jerry became his profession! It was enough for him to emerge only sporadically for a breath of fresh air and this almost always took him to the coast or to the mountains and customarily accompanied only by Susi. Here, Jerry was given to his wildflowers and Susi to her fishing and both were quite content to be alone in their odd togetherness.

Jerry was a philosophical moralist, an ardent champion of justice and of equally shared rights, privileges and responsibilities. Sometimes his strong sense of fairness and shared responsibility spawned amusingly idiosyncratic persuasions. This was the case on my one and only camping trip with Jerry to the Sierras. Without mules, we had to backpack our considerable bulk of gear. Jerry resolved the matter in his usual logical and fair manner. He argued, straight of face, that since the total weight had to be equalized and since he was thirty pounds heavier than I, that his pack should obviously be thirty pounds lighter than mine. This was but another example of Jerry's idiosyncratic ways of coping with problems. To avoid another of our frequent abstruse arguments, I obliged, but only partially, settling for only half of the proposal in view of the long trek ahead of me.

And now just a few more drolleries plus some disquieting proclivities to embellish my disquisition on a favorite eccentric—drolleries and proclivities the likes of which make us the humans that we are. Jerry was not one to do what did not, but for good reason, have to be done. Conventional wisdom regarding the cause and effect relationship between the brushing of teeth and fewer tooth cavities was not wise enough for Jerry. But for the exceptional rare brief brush, he let nature take care of itself and had no great loss since he was genetically blessed with particularly cavity-resistant ivories. Jerry's use of tools was at times even more unorthodox than his nonuse of the toothbrush. With more tasty Gravenstein apples than I can consume, I have annually for many years made, half-baked and frozen up to two dozen or more enormous dome-shaped pies. When I first left one of these behemoths on Jerry's doorstep, he blithely ignored my accompanying reminder to first thaw it and then to finish its baking before cutting and serving it. Deducing that the pie baked whole was likely to become quite stale before he and Susi could consume it, Jerry halved it handily with a rusty old handsaw. Thanks to this characteristically unorthodox Hirschbergian resolution of the problem, one half of the pie could be baked immediately and the other half preserved in the freezer for future baking and neither half had an opportunity to become stale.

Like most humans, Jerry was not averse to permitting himself disquieting idiosyncracies that were both out of keeping with his basic nature and ignored his better judgment. Though by nature and in self-defense an emotionally very contained person, neither envious or malicious, timid rather than assertive and peaceful not bellicose, Jerry the Dr. Jekyll could in sentiment upon occasion become Jerry the Mr. Hyde, a metamorphosis that was all the more startling in its infrequency. Jerry made no secret of his aversion to, and disparagement of Polish Jews, or of his suspicion of, and loathing for Germans, or of his indiscriminate disdain for orthopedists and their too ready recourse to the knife. His brusque advocacy of the death penalty to keep the asocial in line, and his passionate embrace of America's wars in Afghanistan and Iraq and of Israel's bloody struggle with the Palestinians were all no less out of character . . . out of character, to be sure, but not out of keeping with his psychological make-up.

A more characteristic and much more endearing amigo was the Jerry who of a Sunday afternoon would proudly favor his visitor or two with his home-baked package-mix cake, the Jerry who took childlike pride in a small hand-sewn pouch he had himself made from factory-cut leather patches, carefully following accompanying directions, the Jerry who was so elated when the blueberry bush he himself had planted and nurtured deigned to yield a few berries, the pedagogic Jerry who delighted in demonstrating his knot-making skill, in showing precisely how to make a campfire and in enlightening in anatomy and tutoring in calculus, or the healing Jerry for whom pro bono medical service was a moral obligation. Even more endearing was the Jerry of heart-rendering recollections: of tearfully recalled memories of a family in want after a father's premature death, of an extremely anxious childhood, of a loving mother lost to the Nazis, of a desperately lonely studious schoolboy whose only happy pastime were his occasional outings with a troop of Jewish boy scouts, of his anxious but fondly recalled relatively happy years as a refugee-student alone in Marseilles and left to his own resources and of his bewildering and trying first few years in the USA adjusting to yet another language and gradually becoming integrated into yet another culture ... integration yes, but never assimilation, for Jerry had no desire or intent to lose his outsider identity.

It is in such eccentrics as Gerald Hirschberg that human faults and vices, frailties and foibles and strengths and virtues are most clearly silhouetted. By knowing and understanding the Jerrys of life, we learn better to know and understand ourselves. It is for this legacy, no less than for a camaraderie of fifty years, that I am deeply indebted to my dear deceased friend Jerry. Given his givens and what he encountered, Jerry coped exemplarily with self and life. What more can one justly expect?

A Purveyor of Violence

*A*merica and violence are synonymous. Violence is both internally and externally a significant ingredient of the American way of life. Crime in America is higher, murder is more common and prisons are more numerous than in any other industrialized western nation. And America's propensity for violence has become its favorite television entertainment.

Violence for alleged peace, freedom, security and democracy is also the most ready recourse of America's foreign policy. America's history of the past more than 100 years has been left scarred by opportunistic wars.

While peace, freedom and democracy have become America's mantra, preemptive military action has been its reflex tactic. And all this is just and right since America is an "exceptional" nation, with an "exceptional" destiny!

It is quite possible that God's America is actually sick both within and without! Food for thought! But the typical American is not about to reflect upon this possibility.

Fleeting Observations. A Cause for Pause

Appreciation and praise are a balm for the grief of wanting self-esteem.
Achievement and good works are a wellspring of pride and merit.
Love and hatred are the irrational impulses that vitalize life.
Space and time are the inescapable irrealities that blight our fragile human reality.
Envy and malice are the dry rot of relationships.
Respect and compassion are a friendly knock on the door.
Cynicism and bitterness are mortal diseases.
Pain and shame are salutary torment.
Hope and despair are choice, not lot.
Fear and anger are shield and weapon.
Certainty and doubt spell friction.
Understanding and empathy are the mortar of friendship.
Arrogance and humility are both defensive tactics.
That altruism and meism are both rooted in egocentricity does not equate them.
Modesty elevates socially, deprecates personally.
Beauty is less fact than taste.
To genius, moderation is a foreign virtue.
To make war for peace is no less absurd than to make peace for war.
That truths may indeed be relative is no cause for their abandonment.
Belief moves mountains more readily than reason.

America the Beautiful

"The United States is in sore need today of an aristocracy of intellect and service. Because such an aristocracy does not exist in the popular consciousness, we are bending the knee in worship to the golden calf of money.... American democracy will become a laughing stock if it continues to exalt ambitious simpletons.....Complacency and self-satisfaction, coupled with too little knowledge, take high rank among our national traits. America tends to drift on a sea of political incompetence and irresponsibility. As matters stand, we have achieved well-nigh a miracle of unrepresentative government. Intelligent American engagement abroad is to be preferred to isolationism.... The stupendous expenditure on the part of many countries in preparation for war is folly that should cease."

This terse characterization of America in 1931 by Nickolas Murray Butler, President of Columbia University, at the annual Charter Day of the University of California in Berkeley, is no less true of America of 2006. Our business tycoons are still too busy fattening the golden calf to be concerned with the welfare of the many, the many are still uninformed, complacent and self-satisfied, our self-serving politicians continue to wallow in incompetence and corruption and imperialistic preemptive military action has taken precedence over intelligent diplomatic engagement.

As never before, the world of business determines American politics, and in turn, fashions its culture, way of life and foreign policy. As such, our democracy has become something of a laughing stock, no longer a government of, by and for the people, but more correctly, a hard-nosed plutocracy, a business aristocracy no less self-engrossed than the landed aristocracy of the pre-industrial world. So much for President Bush's much-touted American Democracy and America's exceptionalism. President Butler's vision of a better aristocracy of intellect and service was clearly, and unfortunately, a pipe dream. What a shame!

Sic transit gloria Americanae!

The Measure of my Treasure

A sweep of Mary's assets

Credits: gentle, empathic, kind, loving, considerate, moral, diligent, honest, conscientious, organized, competent, sensitive, articulate, thoughtful, altruistic, generous, reflective, frugal.

Debits: hypersensitive to slight, excessively cautious, somewhat paranoid, lacking in self-appreciation, emotionally volatile, too little self-esteem, too dependent emotionally upon the opinion of others, too timid, too much self-doubt, masochistic, too little skilled in interpersonal relationships, plagued by self-doubt and by unwarranted guilt and unwarranted suspicion.

Given these assets Mary's life has been an emotional roller-coaster. Credits and debits have been engaged in a constant tug-of-war. Caught between these positive and negative characteristics and tendencies, Mary cultivated the former diligently and successfully. Her efforts to grapple with her debits were, in contrast, tentatively and decidedly less successful. She failed to come to grips and to terms with her psychological minuses. Avoidance and suppression are no resolution, periodic emotional eruptions were inevitable and the results were painful and damaging. This need not continue to be the case! Debits have only to be reduced in their number and intensity, and that in a painful self-confrontation that can result in a more positive and less painful adjustment to the self and others. But change is in order and possible only if change is desired!

I, for my part, accept and treasure Mary for all her pluses and minuses, for I know she accepts and treasures me and mine!

America's Moral Musts

*I*f America continues to argue exceptionalism, its exceptionalism must be characterized by reciprocity.
If America persists in its interventionist foreign policy, it must intervene diplomatically and not militarily.

If America feels called upon to democratize the world and to spread liberty, it must do so by example and not by force.

If America is to fend off international anger and hate and attract admiration and love, it must live and not just mouth its virtues.

If America is to be the exemplary nation it purports to be, it must improve its public education system, enhance its medical and social care, curb its radical individualism, humanize its capitalism, cleanse its politics and exercise diplomacy rather than war.

If America is to shrink the ever-growing enormous gap between its few rich and its many poor, it must shackle its capitalism and be more generous to its lesser fortunates.

If America, as the world power, is to be more than just a flash across the skies of history, it must forego its imperialism.

If America is to realize its magnificent potential, it must change broadly, drastically and quickly.

The eleventh hour has struck,

Time is running out!

The Power of Fear

Of the many passions that motivate us as human beings, fear ranks among the most compelling. More often than not and almost always to our detriment, we are inclined to counter fear reflexively rather than thoughtfully. Unfortunately, too, fear has always been and still is a commodity in ample supply and readily dispensed to compel acceptance or elicit compliance. While this immoral insinuation of fear can have untoward consequences on the level of the individual or of the group, it can be utterly disastrous on the national political plane. History has witnessed this countless times!

Our naïve president, George W. Bush and his wily entourage of militaristic and empire-minded neo-conservatives are but the latest of national politicians to have recourse to fear to keep the hoi polloi in line and in step and to serve their grandiose nefarious purposes.

Fear, adroitly nurtured and spread by the powers that be, invited and has made onerous hypervigilance palatable to America's population at large. Hypervigilance, in turn, has in the name of national security further stoked the coals of fear, according more license to America's governing myopic apostles and purveyors of American democracy and liberty.

Thanks to fear, born of brash lies and deception bolstered by empty administrative bravado and unwarranted conviction, the majority of Americans acquiesced docilely to an administrative abrogation of treasured constitutionally guaranteed rights, closed their eyes to Bush's background quest of oil control and empire, became compliant accomplices in Bush's possessed foreground pursuit of terrorists allegedly threatening to destroy America and in his furtive and futile wars in Afghanistan and Iraq. America sold its soul to a huckster and for naught but grief!

Such is the power of fear in the hands of the misguided and the unscrupulous.

"The only thing we have to fear is fear itself." Such were the sage words of Franklin D. Roosevelt, a president much wiser than George W. Bush.

The Enigma that is America

On the surface, America is a land of breathtaking promise, endless hope and fantastic dreams.
Beneath the surface lurks angry frustrations, painful despair and bitter disillusionment.
On the surface, America is a land of law and equality.
Beneath the surface lurks rampant crime and widespread racism.
On the surface, America is a land of enormous wealth and grand hospitality.
Beneath the surface lurk widespread poverty and smoldering xenophobia.

Essayistic Ventures and Topical Asides

On the surface, America is a land of peace, brotherhood and good will. Beneath the surface lurk militarism, violence and cavalier indifference.

On the surface, America is a land of democracy of, by and for the people.

Beneath the surface lurks a plutocracy of, by and for the wealthy.

On the surface, America is a land of tranquility and moderation.

Beneath the surface lurk smoldering unrest and threatening passions.

On the surface, America is a land of religion and righteousness.

Beneath the surface lurk secularism and cynicism.

On the surface, America is a land of internationalism, sophistication, glamour and glitter.

Beneath the surface lurk provincialism, conventionality and ordinariness.

On the surface, America is a land of universities, avant-garde scientists and creative thinkers.

Beneath the surface lurk mediocrity, ignorance and aversion to thought.

On the surface, America is a land of freedom, unfettered individualism and unhampered capitalism.

Beneath the surface lurk conformity, gross individual inequities and widespread poverty.

On the surface, America is a land of idealism, morality and spirituality.

Beneath the surface lurk materialism, hedonism and a passion for money.

On the surface, America is a land of good hospitals, competent doctors, enviable medical technology and bounteous drugs.

Beneath the surface lurk inadequate medical care for the poor, wanting preventative medical care, widespread lack of medical insurance and prohibitively expensive prescription drugs.

On the surface, America is a land of noble traditions, of humanity, honor, rectitude and civility, a civilization worthy of emulation.

Beneath the surface lurk a culture of products, consumers, corporate corruption and profits, a social structure that tolerates the exploitation of immigrant workers, the astronomical monetary rewards for its

CEOs and the obscene growing financial gap between the rich and the poor, and perpetuates a political world that exploits the chauvinism it nurtures, sacrifices civil rights to expediency, engages in the "rendition" and torture of presumed terrorists, espouses preemptive military strikes to counter assumed hostile enemy intentions, supports cooperative dictators and effects régime changes when economic advantage so demands and imperialist designs are thereby furthered. America is clearly a billboard enigma in its glaring contradictions. But America is also anything but an exception among nations. Being the present world's superpower, its pluses and minuses are only correspondingly more gargantuan and their contradictions resultantly only that much more disturbing.

Once there were no nations, only warring tribes. Some day, there will again be no nations and hopefully only one grand peaceful united whole. A possibility but not yet a probability!

Our Armageddon

Periodically the world must have its Armageddons.

Periodically the forces of good must be marshaled to combat the forces of evil. This time, America and Co. in the person of self-deemed messianic G. W. Bush, have risen to the occasion to protect Western Christian culture and civilization against a threatening tyrannical Islamic fascism that hates our democracy and liberty and vows to destroy us. G. W. Bush, a buff of history with a flair for drama, has drawn up the lines of battle and has identified the opposing camps and their lineages.

Peering into the not-too-distant past, our informed, perceptive and analytical president wisely fixed his attention upon Democracy's twentieth-century bloody confrontation with totalitarian Nazism, Fascism and Communism and it quickly dawned upon him that America and Co.'s current bloody confrontation with the totalitarian Islamic world is an analogous Armageddon. Bush has wisely observed, and coincidentally to good personal political benefit, that today's Armageddon is but a variation on an old theme. All is as it once was but for a different stage and a change in costumes. He and America and Co. are and are fighting for what Churchill and allies were and fought for, namely leaders and defenders of Democracy and freedom. Bin Laden and his subalterns are but variants of erstwhile dictators Hitler, Mussolini and Stalin, and terroristic Islam is but Nazism, Fascism and Communism in religious garb.

Prompted by this analogy, Bush chose to become for America the single-minded bigoted fear-mongering cheerleader and savior Churchill had been for England. To differ with Churchill's aggressive foreign policy was to be dismissed, as was Neville Chamberlain, as naïve, ill-informed and appeasing. Bush has been no less cavalierly dismissive of the critics of his brash militarism. Churchill was primarily intent upon saving his declining British Empire and he also reveled in his absolute power. Bush is determined to expand his American Empire and he, too, wields his war-time scepter of privilege and power with gusto and abandon. Churchill's military victory was Pyrrhic and the British Empire has gone the way of all preceding empires. Is there reason to believe that our ultimate military victory will be different and that the *Imperium Americanum* will prevail.

Armageddons come and go. Each camp will have its victories and each its defeats, and if these Armageddons continue there will be no end to unnecessary slaughter and destruction. A change of thought and of course is long overdue. Diplomacy, understanding, humanity, patience, tolerance, moderation, and peace deserve their day!

The Changing Face of News

The newspaper was once primarily narrative with the occasional photo. The narrative shrank over the years, the photos multiplied and advertisements began to be featured.

Radio news was once uninterrupted narrative. It has become narrative interspersed liberally with advertisements.

Television news was once primarily narrative, generously laced with photos and only briefly interrupted by verbal advertisements. With the passing of time, narrative became verbal snapshots, splinters and tidbits of information, illustrative photos yielded to actional video, and interruptive advertising became dramatic cinematic interludes.

Common to each of these three means of mass communication has been the gradual shrinking and fragmentation of narrative news and the progressively greater emphasis upon gripping optical imagery. News has clearly become less informative and intellectually challenging, and decidedly more entertaining. This is a clear trivialization of news that leaves a traditionally ill-informed American public less prepared than ever for responsible thought and decision.

News, entertainment and advertisement would do better to go their separate ways!

The Wonders and Want of Verbal Language

What is verbal language but sounds uttered, sounds written or printed, sounds heard, read and understood, a magical transmission of information and thoughts, a meaningful verbal dance in endless variations. Without this marvel—both the most common of our commodities and the most awesome invention of mankind—cultures and civilizations would be unthinkable.

What is language but a communal verbal interaction, a social instrument played by all and mastered by few, a reflection of all that we have been and of all that we are, a measure of our humanity.

What is language but a phenomenon that binds and separates, that energizes and motivates, lethargizes and immobilizes, shatters and destroys, organizes thought and gives direction to actions, inspires and creates.

Essayistic Ventures and Topical Asides

All its wonders notwithstanding, this most marvelous of human constructs, this intricately organized world of symbolic sound is ultimately alarmingly deficient!

A language's concrete nouns, in and out of context, are three dimensional. They are audible, they signify and they are pictorial. *In context:* A woman with a child in her arms and a boy with a dog at her side stood waiting at the curb for a taxi.

Out of context: woman, child, arms, boy, dog, side, curb, taxi.

A language's actional words (verbs, infinitives, participles, actional nouns) fall slightly short of this three-dimensional reach. Like the concrete nouns, these are audible and signify in or out of context, but are pictorial only in context, and then only vaguely. *In context:* The injured runner asked the gathering crowd to disperse.

Out of context: asked, to disperse, injured, gathering, runner.

A language's substitute and qualifying words (personal, reflexive, possessive, demonstrative, interrogative, relative and indefinites pronouns, together with descriptive adjectives and adverbs) are as dimensionally limited as its actional words. Like the latter, these too are only faintly pictorial and only so in context.

In context: The nurse reminded herself that the old doctor, to whom she had referred both those who were seriously injured and others only mildly ill, had always been very accommodating.

Out of context: she, herself, those, who, others, old, seriously.

A language's supplementary words (possessive, demonstrative, interrogative and indefinite adjectives, definite and indefinite articles, auxiliary verbs) and its connectives (prepositions and conjunctions) are audible and signify but are fully blank pictorially in and out of context. This complete loss of one dimension is quite negligible since the words in question are but functional aids in communication.

In context: His publisher sent him these pamphlets and a bill along with the several books he had ordered.

Out of context: his, these, several, the, a, had, with, and.

A language's concrete nouns, combined with its actional, substitute, qualifying and connective words, mirror the tangible world remarkably well. The equally, if not more significant world of abstractions is, in marked contrast, ill-served by a language's considerable body of abstract nouns, sundry verbal enhancements notwithstanding. Abstract nouns (feeling, emotions, anger, sorrow, love, envy, compassion, malice, concept, phenomenon, reason, rationality, God, devil, piety, modesty, charity, evil, grace, goodness, humanity, meditation, forgiveness *et al.*) are as audible as concrete nouns, but unlike their counterparts, they only imply vaguely rather than signify precisely and have absolutely no pictorial dimension. The world of feelings, emotions and idea, the more ethereal, subtle, and elusive area of human expertise, is short-changed by its related words. The very stuff of life is left beyond the pale of language. The essence of abstract terminology eludes us and our resort, to date, to the approximations of analogy or to explanatory qualifiers has been but a gauche flailing.

A language of words clearly served caveman better than it does modern man. Some day in the evolution of mankind a new, non-verbal mode of communication, one able to deal directly and fully with feelings, emotions and ideas, may yet evolve to supplement our present magnificent yet painfully inadequate language of words.

It was such a possibility that Goethe may have had in mind when he intimated: "Liebe spricht in Tönen, denn Gedanken sind zu fern." ("Love speaks in tones, for thoughts are too remote.")

Alienation and the Slight Syndrome

The world is rapidly succumbing to a new plague, the hypersensitivity-to-slight syndrome.

Pope Benedict had only to quote a negative remark about Muhammed by a fourteenth-century Byzantine emperor to set the Muslims of Turkey afire. An American comedian had only to shout the n-word while on stage to infuriate Black America's leaders. Crosses on a hillside to remind Americans of the number of their fallen soldiers in Iraq caused enough controversy to make newspaper headlines for days. A four-foot wreath-shaped peace-on-earth symbol in front of a home was enough to stir the wrath of neighbors convinced that the display was politically divisive or even a sign of the devil. Any public questioning of Israel's subjugation of the Palestinians or any expression of sympathy for the latter is customarily followed by a stream of angry letters to the editor by outraged Jews. Muslim garb has become offensive enough in such countries as France, Germany and Holland to persuade legislators to pass laws restricting its use in public. Incidents such as these, largely spawned by alienation have become ubiquitous!

Alienation of whatever kind commonly hatches suspicion and fear that all too frequently become paranoia, which in turn, characteristically breeds malice, and malice exercised inevitably angers its victims and spawns in them a persistent hypersensitivity-to-slight that demands redress. An emotionally healthy individual, like an emotionally healthy society, can tolerate the slings and arrows of outrageous fortune without becoming psychologically afflicted. Unfortunately our unstable world comprises an ever growing number of societies and individuals on the edge emotionally and unable to deal with their circumstances of life with equanimity.

Society has world-wide become a motley array of conflicting, disparaging, self-conscious, hypersensitive and trigger-happy factions or "tribes" possessed by one cause or another: race, ethnicity, religion, politics, gender, sex *et al.* Intertribal slurs and slights have devastating consequences, and typically at the drop of a hat. There is, furthermore, no dearth of alienation and strife within society's contentious factions. Indeed, sundry groups, families and even individuals interrelate no differently.

The interactive lot of the world's many disparate, hypersensitive and slight-shy societies is, in cause and effect, but a variation of the hypersensitive interaction of the factions and sub-factions of any given society.

Given the ubiquity of our age's multi-level alienation and its untoward effects, and but for drastic change in human thought and behavior, our world is likely to become a mélange of moated fortresses, and the individual an island unto himself, armed and ready. This may already be the case!

G. W. Bush's Brash Pronunciamentos

"Iraq clearly has weapons of mass destruction and threatens America and the free world" was long Bush's insistent mantra. This was but a deliberate lie to justify the war!

Standing proud on a battleship, Bush joyously announced "mission accomplished." It clearly was not!

Repeatedly Bush has maintained that "Iraq, thanks to America, is now free and a democracy." Neither is yet the case!

With smirking Rumsfeld at his side, Bush jovially proclaimed that he was proud of his minister of defense and would stand by him. Rumsfeld was fired the next day!

Bush has repeatedly asserted his confidence in and support of Iraq's faltering Prime Minister Maliki. Maliki has good cause for worry, as had Rumsfeld!

Bush has not ceased to repeat his brash battle cries: "We will not cut and run; we will stay the course until our mission is accomplished." What will this prove to be but typical perverse Bushian bravado that presages the opposite!

Verbally George W. Bush is a riddle, albeit less than a perplexing challenge. He says what he means to say, and at that moment wants to and seems to believe what he is saying. When his beliefs change, and they do so as rapidly as changing circumstances dictate and Karl Rove advises, then his pronunciamentos change accordingly and unabashedly. Bush's added bravado and bluster are but juvenile manner to lend more credence to his labile beliefs. To be mindful of these idiosyncrasies of thought and word is to preclude surprises!

85th Birthday Celebration

May 28, 2007

Ecclesiastics: Chapter 3

For everything there is a season, and a time to every purpose:
A time to be born, and a time to die,
A time to plant, and a time to harvest,
A time to weep, and a time to laugh,
A time to mourn, and a time to dance,
A time to get and a time to lose,
A time to rend and a time to sew,
A time to love and a time to hate,
A time for war and a time for peace . . .

We would all do well to be mindful of these injunctions, and particularly of the last three. To rend, to hate and to fight have always come naturally and plentifully, to sow, to love and to be peaceful have always required nurturing and have, therefore, remained rarer interactions. Each of us can help change this imbalance for the better, and we can do so, if each of us patches up whatever has been torn, lets appreciation replace animosities and sees to it that friendly and not belligerent interactions prevail.

I would like to add my own reminder to the quoted biblical injunctions: There is a time to be thankful and to rejoice—a fitting addendum, particularly for me upon the occasion of my 85th birthday. I am happy and thankful for these 85 years, for these privately and professionally very satisfying years. I am also happy about and thankful for the family that sprang up around me. Children and grandchildren have made a wonderful difference in my life. I hope that I have added a positive dimension to theirs. You have been and are the ballast of my life. Without you, life would have been and would be rather bleak. I thank you!

Let's hope that five years from now we will all again gather to celebrate and to give thanks.

Politicians: Slogans, Lies and Semantics

*P*oliticians are in general not inclined to inform or to clarify, and for good reason. This instructive recourse presupposes well-grounded and clearly defined worthy undertakings or policies, demands patience and time and results more often than not in a diversity of opinion rather than in an unqualified acceptance of the proposed. Since most weighty political matters are more grand scheme than detailed program and since time is almost always of the essence and controversy is best avoided, a tactic other than instructive persuasion has clearly been in order.

Keen students of human inclinations that they are, our world's politicians have also long noted that most of their lesser fellow humans respond more readily and more favorably to simple assertions expressed briefly than to thought-demanding exegetic wordiness. Little wonder that slogans became their mantras and particularly so in times of crises. Such has been no less the case in America. In his contribution to this dubious but effective mode of persuasion, George W. Bush did more than just fall in line and keep in step. Wanting in language skills, he came into his own in a stubborn cultivation of slogans. Two causes were thereby well-served: catch phrases not only afforded an effective political language but also helped him compensate for his obvious ineptitude in normal communication. Indeed, Bush's naturally disjointed, telegrammatic mode of thinking may also have found a consonant mode of expression in the halting and broken flow of slogan language.

The favorite of Bush's litany of slogans have been: Iraq's arsenal of weapons of mass destruction threatens the U.S.A.; Hussein's harboring of branches of Bin Laden's Al Qaeda poses a world-wide threat; we will bring Democracy and Freedom to Iraq; we will not cut and run; we will stay the course; we will succeed unless we quit; we will stand down as they stand up; we are winning, we will win; we will lead the world to freedom. With the exception of his references to weapons of mass destruction, to the threat of terrorism and to Democracy and Freedom, all of Bush's favorite mantras, unqualified as they have remained, are clearly nothing more than simplistic jingoistic pep talk.

Deliberately stoking fear of nuclear and chemical weapons of mass destruction and fear of Islamic terrorism, Bush was able to persuade the majority of his fellow Americans to condone his pre-emptive invasion of Iraq. That Iraq proved to have no weapons of mass destruction and that Bin Laden and his evil and freedom-hating Islamic terrorists had never played footsie with Hussein never morally ruffled Bush or any member of his entourage of tough-fibered neo-conservatives. That such could have been the case was enough to justify a pre-emptive strike. Furthermore, once lies have served their purpose, they should conveniently be forgotten. This had become Bush's *modus operandi*.

Bush's evangelistic insistence that it was God's will that America gift Iraq, indeed the entire world, with Democracy and Freedom, was no less a deliberate self-serving verbal camouflage than his weapons of mass destruction. Laudable pretext, like weapon lie, served its purpose predictably well. Most of America's many God-fearing citizens believed, or wanted to believe, their president, and supported their country's noble crusade, and the doubters–those who knew or suspected that Bush and his neo-conservatives were actually less interested in lofty causes than in the removal of a regime that no longer served America's political purposes, in the establishment of an imperialistic foothold in Islam's troubled Middle East and in the control of Iraq's oil fields–chose discreetly to maintain their silence, that is, until sociopolitical chaos enveloped Iraq. By then too, the words Democracy and Freedom had, self-servingly for Bush and his entourage, slipped in meaning from their initially implied high expectations to nothing more than a government able to govern and to provide security. This semantic slippage, a determined effort to save face and to failure-proof, became a White House trend with Iraq's decline from chaotic strife to civil war.

The American army's lightning thrust did awe and shock, Hussein's puny army folded in a matter of weeks, and Bush in military garb and on a battleship off the Pacific coast–a grand Hollywoodesque photo opportunity–smiling smugly, proclaimed "mission accomplished." This, unfortunately, was nothing other than the beginning of the stream of brash lies, pious hopes and deliberate semantic slippage that was to follow as matters in Iraq quickly went from bad to worse.

Despite Iraq's increased sectarian friction, the escalation of terrorism and the rapidly growing number of American and Iraqi casualties, Bush, bolstered by Karl Rove, Dick Cheney and Donald Rumsfeld, continued to reiterate his favorite cheerleader slogans, albeit with less gusto and shifting emphasis. In reaction to America's growing disapproval of his imperiled Iraqi adventure, Bush's once emphatically proclaimed "we will not cut and run" gave way in emphasis to a more modest and accommodating "we will stand down as they stand up," and his once stubbornly maintained "we will stay the course" became an acknowledgment of the necessity of "a change in tactics." "We will stand down as they stand up," Bush's new slogan, both slyly threw that ball of responsibility into the court of the Iraqis and conveniently lowered the definition of victory. And Bush's "change in tactics" fuzzily defined by his new and self-cancelling catchwords "consistency" and "flexibility" demonstrated his characteristic lack of respect for the intelligence of the American people.

Bush's lack of respect for the intelligence of the American public is reflected even more in his consistent devious use of language. Emotionally distressing or morally unacceptable situations or acts are commonly wrapped in innocuous verbal camouflage. By designating questionable civilians enemy combatants, the White House legitimized its illegal imprisonments in Guantanamo; the kidnapping, spiriting abroad, torture and interrogation of alleged terrorists became "extraordinary renditions"; torturing suspects to obtain confessions became "information extraction"; a life-threatening dunking to compel confessions simply became "water boarding"; the killing of civilians and the destruction of non-military properties customarily became "collateral damage"; unpopular military escalation became a less offensive "surge"; and sharply defined "victory" and "defeat" became blander and less specific "success" and "failure." Clearly, to further befuddle and not to enlighten, Bush's pro-war arguments in time began to be peppered indiscriminately with such non-defined pseudo-technical terms as road-map, timetables, milestones and benchmarks, and even such commonplace words as win, lose, success, hero, patriotism, justice, friend, foe, torture and terrorism became self-servingly elusive in their meaning. This verbal campaign was remarkably successful in its intended rousing of the emotions and the stultifying of the wits of a majority of Americans for more than three years.

With disaster staring him in the face after three years of combat, Bush continued to insist that America would succeed unless it quit and that it was in fact winning in Iraq. But the words "success" and "winning" changed semantically, and for good reason: the possibility of the Democracy and Freedom once envisaged and promised had become a virtual impossibility. And Bush's latest brash and shifty pronunciamentos—we are going to stay in Iraq to finish the job; we will stay as long as our friends the Iraqis want us to stay; victory in Iraq is crucial to the defeat of terrorism, the calling of our time; we want to continue to work with the sovereign government of Iraq and we will achieve our mutual aims; to leave before finishing the job is to dishonor those who have sacrificed the lives for a just cause; Al Qaeda is on the rise; they can't intimidate America; victory is still achievable–are little more than the desperate ranting and pleading of a man who suspects that all will soon be lost.

Regarding Iraq, America's cause, reasons, planning and leadership were all wrong. Our hopes, fed by empty promises and edged by cultivated fear, were pie in the sky. We have been fighting a bogus war on two fronts–with devious slogans on the home front and with devastating weapons in Iraq–and after almost four years of fumbling and bumbling we are still mired in political and military muck. Like Vietnam, Iraq was clearly a misadvised misadventure. Vietnam ended in a costly disaster and Iraq is ending in a costly disaster–calamities for both invader and invaded. More than three thousand American soldiers have already lost their lives in Iraq, more than twenty thousand have already been wounded, the war has already cost America hundreds of billions of dollars and American has lost the respect of the world at large. And Iraq has become a dangerous wasteland, more than six hundred thousand of its citizens have been slaughtered, and several million have become displaced persons. All this for at best, a Pyrrhic American victory, or at worst, another humiliating American defeat.

So much for America's self-righteous flag-waving and gun-toting imperialism, so much for the deceptive sleight-of-word artistry of politicians and so much for the naïve trust and gullibility of the American people. How many more Pied Piper deciders will seduce America? How many more asinine ventures are necessary before adolescent America becomes mature?

Hope springs eternal in the human breast! The floundering ship that is America may yet right itself!

Adult Infancy and Cultural Decline

Adult infancy, America's insatiable appetite for entertainment of whatever ilk—both likely cause and byproduct of cultural decline—has of late been spreading like wildfire. How else is one to account for our puppy-love affair with Hollywood and its questionable celebrities, for our addiction to television's plethora of soppy soap operas and boisterous reality shows, for our juvenile obsession with sports and our immature idolization and outrageous remuneration of our baseball, basketball and football heroes, for such popular public peek-shows and trivial fascinations as the Anna Nicole Smith escapade, the capers of Paris Hilton and Britney Spears, the Jerry Springer serial exposure of imbecilic human behavior, the voyeuristic attraction of television's ever more titillating display of scantily-dressed females and the general vicarious delight in its violence *ad nauseam,* for America's joyful preoccupation with electronics gadgetry, for the Steve Job absurd iPhone hoopla and for our pleasure-filled consumerism. All this spells deliberate self-blinding infantile entertainment, and all this recalls Emperor Nero who, like a self-indulgent child, chose to close his eyes and fiddle blithely while Rome burned.

Cultural decline marks a return to an original morass, a shedding of cultural apparel no longer appealing. America's unraveling—but a chapter in the decline of Western Civilization—like that of Ancient Rome, is unmistakably characterized by the opiate revelry of entertainment, by adult infancy!

Three is More than Three

But an ordinary number, to begin with, three in time and in its ever broader more figurative use gradually transcended itself and became a tantalizing concept and a conspicuous presence in the folklore of the Western World. This particularizing of three began with religion (the three Holy Kings of Epiphany; Christ denied thrice by Peter; Christ's resurrection on the third day after his crucifixion; the Trinity; the three virtues: faith, hope and charity), became widespread in literature (R. Southey, *The Three Bears*; A. Dumas, *The Three Musketeers*; A. Chekhov *The Three Sisters*; P. Alarcón, *The Three-Cornered Hat*; B. Brecht, *The Threepenny Opera*), took early hold in art (the triptych altarpiece; Three Philosophers by Giorgione; Three Crosses by Rembrandt; Three Musicians by Picasso), found its way into politics (America's executive, legislative and judicial branches of government; France's *liberté, égalité* and *fraternité*; Latvia's Order of Three Stars; triumvirate et triarchy), into games (three of a kind in poker; three-cushion billiards; Tic Tac Toe, Ready Set Go, Paper Sticks and Stones; baseball's three strikes and three outs) into music (the waltz in triple time; three sections of the sonata form) and into nursery rhymes (Three blind mice, Three little kittens, Three men in a tub, Three bags of wool) and became ubiquitous in the world of fairytales (three wishes, three guesses, three chances, three tasks, three bears, three billy goats gruff, three little pigs).

The number seven has fascinated the Western World no less than has three. A few random examples are enough to show that it, too, has acquired a patina of magic: the seven days of creation, the seven last words of Christ, the seven deadly sins, the seven virtues, seventh heaven, Seventh-Day Adventists, Seven Pillars of Wisdom; seven days of the week, seven wonders of the world, Seven Seas, the Seven Hills of Rome; seven-card stud poker, lucky seven or eleven in dice gambling; seven-year itch.

This peculiarly extended use of such numbers as three and seven (and to these could be added nine, eleven and thirteen) is but one of the many oddities of language in action. A language's figures of speech (metaphor, allegory, simile, euphemism, metonymy, synecdoche *et al.*) are probably the most common, the most intricate and the most striking of these language eccentricities.

Bush and Hitler: Disturbing Similarities

*H*itler was an arrogant man, proud and theatrically pompous, stupidly stubborn and insufferably self-righteous. George W. Bush is all that and only in slight variation.

Hitler was the self-anointed infallible "Führer" of his nation, and Bush is America's self-crowned cocksure "decider."

Hitler dreamed of a German Empire, of "Lebensraum" and security for his people, and Bush envisaged an American Empire secure in its Homeland Defense and in its control of the world's oil reserves. And for both, war was the means to these ends.

Those who opposed Hitler's persecution of the Jews and his military misadventures were branded enemies of the fatherland, and those who take umbrage at Bush's violation of civil rights and question Bush's justification of his invasion of Iraq are summarily dismissed as Un-American. Patriotism has for Bush been no less a weapon to fend off criticism than it was for Hitler.

Hitler duplicitously maintained that he was less intent upon conquest than upon spreading the blessings of German culture and of the German way of life to Europe's lesser nations, and Bush would

Essayistic Ventures and Topical Asides

have us believe that his wars are primarily intent upon spreading America's prized democracy and liberty throughout the world. This self-proclaimed mission of Bush is no less a Christian conceit than Hitler's pan-Germanic mission was a Teutonic conceit. Hitler argued German exceptionalism and Bush has continued to argue American exceptionalism.

It is interesting to note, and anything but a coincidence, that Bush's inner entourage of fellow-bigoted and bellicose neo-conservative colleagues and advisors (Dick Cheney, Donald Rumsfeld, Paul Wolfowitz, Richard Perle, William Kristol, David Frum) is reminiscent of Hitler's inner circle of sinister and obdurate Nazi cronies (Josef Goebbels, Hermann Göring, Alfred Rosenbaum, Heinrich Himmler, Rudolf Hess).

Hitler left utter havoc in his wake!

Is it surprising that Bush is leaving widespread disaster in his wake!

War ad nauseam

The American public has been on a prolonged military diet—a combined consumption of the present wars in Afghanistan/Iraq and of the past Second World War—a regimen that has left it politically divided, confused and on edge.

Afghanistan and Iraq have for years been troubling menus dished out daily by the media. This daily soap-opera-like fare was augmented by a flurry of Second-World-War documentaries—among them, *America in the Forties, California at War, The War: Nisei Soldiers, Beyond the Medal of Honor,* and Walter Cronkite's recall of the Allies' defeat of Hitler's Germany—gripping experiences ranging in length from a half hour to three hours. All this military fanfare was then topped by the filmmaker Ken Burn's moving panoramic view of the entire Second World War, a buffet feast of some fifteen hours: seven military banquets twice on display in but eleven days!

The subject matter and grand sweep of Burn's chef d'oeuvre, *The War*, cannot help but recall Tolstoi's masterpiece, *War and Peace*. Burn's amalgam of actual news films accompanied by narration was seven years in its making, focusses on America and war from 1939 to 1945 and it radically extended the epic possibilities of the documentary. Tolstoi's freewheeling narrative some six years (1863–68) in its writing, with its focus on Russia and war, broadened the epic range of the traditional novel. Unfortunately, similarities end with these parallels. Tolstoi, seeker, moralist and philosopher, was preoccupied with the human condition. His oeuvre rises above its material to illustrate the ultimate interrelatedness of all life. No comparable existential comment is implied by Burn's cinematized documentary. The filmmaker remained a filmmaker with his eye on his fellow countrymen and on the box office, a good patriot with considerable tolerance for war and a less than subtle propagandist, and his recall of a past Armageddon became a paean to America, its heroic pursuit of a horrific war that was deemed necessary, good and just, an agony that ended in deserved victory. Dire actuality became attractive soothing myth!

By featuring the war in all its immensity and horror only in brief spells, ever shifting his focus from battlefield to battlefield in Europe, the Pacific and Japan, by alternating individual heroics on the battlefield and the homefront, by constantly interweaving the testimonials of individual soldiers from specific typical American communities, by interspersing stirring newspaper reports and radio broadcasts of the time, by adding a steady flow of connective editorial comment and by providing a background of sentimental wartime songs, Burns manages both to attenuate and to make palatable the slaughter and devastation of the war and to hold his viewers spellbound. With adroit recourse to these cinematic tactics, Burns is able to entertain, to make a strong patriotic statement and to present a veiled apology for war.

Burn's subjective cinematizing of events rather than objective chronicling of facts makes for good patriotic drama but poor history. The same holds true of the additional war documentaries mentioned earlier.

How are such documentaries likely to impact the public? Will they serve their intended patriotic purposes or will they, and particularly *The War*, like most gripping television fare, be no more than an immediate affirmative fix or a negative downer, both soon forgotten? The latter is most likely to be the case.

Those who are against the war in Iraq or opposed to war in general, are likely to brush *The War* off as but more inane war-mongering. Diehard patriots, ever ready to take up arms for their country, will undoubtedly be confirmed in their conviction that our country is always right and that our wars are always justified. And those, probably the many, who are not particularly patriotic nor particularly averse to America's involvement in wars, will probably continue to sit silently on the sidelines. Time will tell!

Interest in war has not been confined to the entertainment and propaganda of the documentaries. Fortunately, the two published volumes of Rick Atkinson's monumental *Libertarian Trilogy* and David Halberstam's impressive *The Cold Winter: America and the Korean War* have added thorough objective scholarship to the prevailing fluff of the documentaries. Unfortunately, since the general public is far more likely to watch documentaries than to grapple with sizeable scholarly-written books, Atkinson and Halberstam are not likely to blunt the thrust of the documentaries.

Is this recent documentary surge in the celebration of war but an innocent coincidence, but a snowball accumulating bulk as it tumbles downhill, or a desperate orchestrated effort by America's arch-nationalist and bellicose neo-conservative republicans to help bolster the country's flagging support of war? Hopefully this surge in either case will be little more than a basking in nostalgia and will be no more successful in its basic intent than our latest military surge in Iraq. In either case, it is best that we respectfully remember the 60 million lives lost in the allegedly necessary and honorable Second World War and that we simultaneously forswear war as a means to an end, even a laudable end! War is not and has never been a solution, it only exacerbates immediate problem and sows the seeds of future problems.

No Want of Nefarious Subterfuge

Egypt

America gives Egypt two billion dollars a year. Officially, to sow the seeds of democracy there. In fact, to buy Egypt's cooperation in the furtherance of America's political and economic interests in the Islamic Mideast!

Israel

America gives Israel three billion dollars a year. Officially, to bolster the only democracy in the Mideast. In fact, to have a strong military foothold on the oil-rich and less than friendly Muslim world!

Iraq

America invaded Iraq and laid it waste. Officially, to destroy its weapons of mass destruction and bless its people with democracy and freedom. In fact, to curb Iraq's growing power in the Mideast and to get control of its oil reserves!

Pakistan

America has been giving Pakistan two billion dollars a year since 2001. Officially, to help President Musharraf promote democracy in his feudal state. In fact, to induce Musharraff to assist America in its faltering efforts to neutralize the Taliban, thereby to help further America's political interests in Afghanistan.

The word democracy appears to have become but a front to camouflage and to lend legitimacy to questionable political purposes. And to what degree has this ploy been successful? To a remarkable degree despite lamentable results! The democracy lure definitely made covert bribery, military action and failure more palatable to a credulous general public. This cross section of the American public simply chose to close its eyes in belief to the cost in money, lives and reputation and to the dismal failure of these misadventures. And fail they did!

Egypt has remained an autocracy, has been less than an obliging ally and continues to laugh all the way to the bank!

Israel's annual windfall has enabled it to continue its destructive control of the Palestinians independent of America's wishes, and America's foothold in the Mideast has become a powder keg!

Iraq lies wasted, democracy is no longer a pressing issue, and the oil fields continue to be out of America's reach!

And Pakistan, with Musharaff's declaration of dictatorial emergency rule (November 2007), has become less democratic and more autocratic than ever, the Taliban is as strong as ever, and that America's political interests in Afghanistan have been furthered is more pious hope than reality!

The means have been abominable, the ends abysmal!

La Condition Humaine

*F*iguratively speaking, most people have always lived content in a vast valley, edged by a huge mountain. A restless few—thinkers and artists of whatever ilk—have always been fascinated by the looming mountain and have always been determined to scale it. Heroic sacrifice and efforts notwithstanding, no one has ever conquered the mountain. Century after century, climbers have managed to struggle ever higher but the mountain peak has always loomed no less remote in its shroud of mist.

This appears to be mankind's lot. The many will continue to live content in the valley, and the few will continue to exhaust themselves in their futile efforts to reach the mountain's peak, a Shangri-la with its treasure trove of absolutes beyond human reach: wisdom, truth and beauty.

Though absolutes have always been beyond mankind's grasp, efforts to achieve the impossible have not been the absurd ordeal of Sisyphus in Hades. The latter's ordeal, forever to push a huge stone up a hill only to have it roll down again, was painful punishment and nothing more. In contrast, the voluntary painful efforts of thinkers and artists to climb ever higher to achieve the impossible have not only been valiant but have had a fruitful result: culture and civilization!

The Baby Boomers and their Resourcefulness

Our enterprising Baby Boomers have been to our society what leaven is to dough. The body first became their focus, fitness their gospel, healthy longevity their hope, and the athletic gym their temple. Determination and resourcefulness paid off, and doubly so. The Boomers enjoyed a physically rigorous middle age and the myriad fitness centers that mushroomed across the country enjoyed their financial take.

And now that their life's twilight has set in, the Baby Boomers are as determined to cope with old age's mental infirmities as capably as they had tended to their bodies. What better than to add mind gyms to their body gyms! A new entrepreneurial opportunity surfaced. Computer software programs and video games to sharpen the flagging mind and to counter Alzheimer's disease soon proved popular and profitable. A brain fitness industry has now been added to the old body fitness business. It promises to become as popular and profitable as its antecedent, but will it be as beneficial? The jury has yet to submit its verdict!

To be sure, what is done in either gym can be done as effectively and decidedly more cheaply at home and outdoors!

Absolutism and Relativity

Ours is an age of growing doubt about our Western Judeo-Christian culture, its traditional beliefs, truths and values. Responses to this cultural crisis are primarily one of two extremes.

Some, in their growing doubt, become progressively more anxious, cling ever more frantically to all that was once absolute and unassailable, and become ever more intolerant of all else that is. They become the true knowers and believers, and their condemnation of the different is absolute. Our Christian evangelicals and sundry fundamentalists exemplify this group.

Others plagued by doubt become progressively more understanding and tolerant of the different and find their solace in the relativity of all beliefs, truths and values. These are our cultural thinkers.

In its absolutism, the first of these groups, knows only battle to sustain its world and to vanquish the threatening foe. For them, an eventual Armageddon is the resolution.

In its relativity, the second group is intent upon mutual understanding, tolerance and entente.

What pertains to and is true of our Western culture pertains to and is no less true of the Muslim World. Both cultures are in decline, both are suffering its pangs and both are reacting frantically and similarly.

The Actual and the Spiritual

*M*ankind has never been content just to wallow thoughtlessly in reality's mucky mess. Human beings have always sought explanations for, and relief from their wanting selves and their wanting world. They have always found explanation and relief in the notion of a better, a spiritual self, and a better, a spiritual world. This belief in a spiritual realm beyond the physical world has always, in due time, become a religion providing expected elucidation and solace. Religion, in turn and in time, and thanks to belief's eventual and inevitable paling and demise, has always become a dated social institution, leaving mankind at a loss again, and again anxious to seek explanation and relief in a new belief. New belief has always been but a variant of old belief and the former's lot has always been but a repetition of the latter's.

This cycle is likely to continue just as long as mankind and the world remain essentially what they have always been!

America that was and America that is

*T*he USA was once an exemplary national possibility, almost a mythical nation that held the world in thrall. That was once upon a time!

Following the Second World War, America gradually metamorphosed from a Dr. Jekyll to a Mr. Hyde. A good citizen of the world became an arrogant, self-serving rogue nation bent upon empire building. Vice replaced virtue and world-wide love and envy became world-wide disdain and hatred.

Hypocrisy has become the order of the day in the foreign policy of the USA. America now preaches democracy but acts autocratically, extols peace but wages war, argues equality but touts its exceptionalism, does not cooperate and prefers to manipulate, does not negotiate and is given to dictate.

Little wonder that our once internationally beloved America has become the world's evil empire.

Sic transit gloria mundi!

Culture, a Fortuitous Byproduct

*C*ulture is but a byproduct of mankind's passion for explanation and need for solace. This passion and need have always spawned belief and belief has always become a religion with final answers and comforting solace, and every religion has always given birth to a companion culture. Religions, too, have always run their sustaining courses and ended in the disarray of disbelief and of concomitant cultural dissolution. And with this inevitable collapse, mankind has always, in due time, begun anew to try to still its passion for explanation and its need for solace in yet another religion and its culture. Our Western Christian Culture has reached this twilight stage. The Western World that we have known is dying and another may already be birthing! What lies ahead?

Politics and Persuasion

War-time politicians learned long ago that bald truth or unvarnished lies are by and large counterproductive. It also became quickly apparent to them that a positive veil of detracting metaphors, assuaging euphemisms and enticing hyperbole is a more effective means of concealment and of persuasion. President Bush and his entourage of crafty neo-conservatives have been no less aware of this political reality than had been Adolf Hitler and his shady inner circle. And the White House's steady flow of up-beat pronouncements has to date been just as effective as Hitler's rousing propaganda had been. In instances such as these, all is always well, but only as long as the politicians' verbal sweeteners are able to lull the public into complacency and acceptance. But credulity has its limits and harsh reality eventually intrudes and all hell breaks out.

According to a smiling and smirking George Bush, America has a messianic mission to fight evil and to bless the world with democracy and freedom. As such, our many wars are laudable, indeed morally necessary crusades. We wage war for peace and that makes their painful inhumanity acceptable. Ours is a humane pin-point bombing and not traditional abhorrent saturation bombing with its resultant indiscriminate devastation.

A "desert storm" that will "shock and awe" is clearly more humane and therefore more acceptable than an invasion that kills and lays waste. Collateral damage makes indiscriminate destruction of property and wanton slaughter of civilians quite impersonal and very palatable. A hapless pause in military operations has become a period of deliberate and advisable consolidation and evaluation. Defeats are masqueraded as strategic retreats. And a war intensified to stave off defeat became more acceptable as a euphemistic surge.

In today's America, verbal sweeteners such as the above have become as common in its world of politics as they were in Nazi Germany's. Persuasion has become dependent upon sweet evasion. Germany paid a horrible price for this vice. What awaits America?

Joseph Mileck   41

Our Light and Dark Worlds

*C*hristianity's mission has been to protect mankind against the devil and his dark world and to save mankind for God and his light realm. Christianity's promises and threats, which over the centuries have at times been more successful and at other times less effective, have, since the industrial revolution, become progressively less persuasive and the dark world has become correspondingly more luring. This trend is culminating in the present incipient cultural decline of the Western World. The dark half of life and all that is associated with it—disbelief, inhumanity, war, crime, violence, nihilism, greed, animality, egocentricity, sexual debauchery, the grotesque, revolting, distorted, lurid, outlandish, ugly, bad, immortal etc.—has become more attractive than the light half of life and all that it has represented—belief, humanity, spirituality, peace, love, sexual continence, pity, compassion, benevolence, brotherhood, kindness, charity, understanding, respect, altruism, moderation, tolerance etc.

We are approaching an end, paradoxically the morass of the beginning, the formless chaos from which our Western Christian Culture emerged. And from this approaching morass, a new culture will in due time gradually emerge, as did ours, and then run its similar cycle.

Word and Action at Variance

*S*ince the Second World War, America has perpetrated violence galore, and all in the name of freedom and democracy. In the West, a series of military intrusions began with Panama, followed by Grenada and Nicaragua. In the East, combat began with Korea, followed by Vietnam, Somalia, Afghanistan and Iraq. At the same time, America installed a flow of dictators in countries from Chile to Zaire.
All this while touting freedom and democracy!
And it all began with a new-born democracy's freedom to enslave!
Civilized externally, America has at heart remained a paradoxical brute!
Hypocrisy lives on!

The Paradox of Politics

Since the end of the Second World War, America and Russia have been checkmating each other at every turn of their political ways. A grim game of diplomatic chess, played at times behind dark curtains, then quite openly, and upon occasion, both secretly and publicly! Georgia, the latest site of confrontation, recalls the Serbian altercation of but a short time ago. Secession was the point of contention in Serbia and secession is again the rub in Georgia. Kosovo seceded from Serbia and South Ossetia and Abkhazia are determined to liberate themselves from Georgia. America and Russia took opposing sides in the Serbian fray, and they are again at predictable loggerheads in the Georgian scuffle. Geopolitics determined America's support of little Kosovo's struggle for independence and no less Russia's support of Big Brother Serbia, and geopolitical concerns determined a paradoxical reversal of roles in Georgia: America's alliance with Big Brother Georgia and Russia's alliance with tiny break-away South Ossetia and equally tiny separatist-minded Abkhazia.

Such are the vicissitudes of politics. Advantage, not morality, is the name of the game, notwithstanding virtuous arguments to the contrary! Neither America nor Russia have been beyond nefarious ulterior motives.

Freedom, a Challenge

Freedom has its many open doors, its many privileges and responsibilities, its many temptations and demands, and its many successes and failures. It can be exhilaration and blessing, seduction and license, or burden and curse. Freedom is an exhilarating circumstance that gives loose rein to possibility, to any possibility.

In keeping with human nature, freedom has left both a questionable and an admirable trail in its wake. While these trails differ somewhat country to country, they are almost consistently more disheartening than encouraging. In America freedom brought with it our very admirable unhampered thought, speech, religion and movement, but has also culminated in our very questionable radical individualism, hedonism, materialism and consumerism. On balance more grief than joy, more swamp than oasis. A pity!

Xenophobia I

*N*igger is to Negro what
Kike is to Jew
Wop is to Italian
Frog is to Frenchman
Chink is to Chinese
Jap is to Japanese
Chirper is to Englishman
Gook is to Vietnamese.
Foul epithets such as these—and there are many more of them—are born of the suspicion, fear and hatred of the stranger. A hostile response to the different other that may once have been necessary in man's struggle for survival is today decidedly more counterproductive than self-preserving. Xenophobia has outlived its *raison d'être!*

National Presidential Conventions

*T*he Democratic and Republican national conventions to select presidential candidates have long been, and are likely to remain more partisan hoopla than serious political engagement. This year's quadrennial party round-ups were no exception.

Each gathering of the faithful was a theatrically-staged extravaganza, an occasion for customary raucous partisan celebration, chauvinistic touting of patriotism, lavish praise of the military and for crowd-pleasing rousing mutual denigration. Neither gathering

Essayistic Ventures and Topical Asides

suffered for want of loud self-adulation and both camps gave moderation and sober bipartisan political thought short shrift. Indeed, each camp was decidedly more circus bravado than assembly-hall sobriety, more grand spectacle than significant event.

Like most presidential conventions, our latest afforded the politicos a relished opportunity to be loud and expansive in their partisan bigotry and a venue for the gathered party loyal to shout their enthusiastic approval. And shout their wild approval to a steady flow of half-truths, outrageous misrepresentation and soap-opera biography both camps did, and with gusto. In each case, too, a parade of party barkers was accompanied by a fanfare of touching videos and sentimental music, and climaxed in carnavalesque song, dance, balloons and confetti.

Both political conventions were as much theater as television's popular pseudo-reality shows and soap operas. Indeed, they were a blend of the two. Rousing entertainment! Manner more than matter! America got what America wants and not what America needs and deserves.

America's Democracy

*D*emocracy in the USA has travelled a rough road, and for many reasons. Neither the structure nor the *modus operandi* of our government is consonant with the spirit of Democracy, nor have the governed many or the governing few been up to the personal demands of Democracy, nor has our American culture been in sync with Democracy.

Candidates for the presidency are not democratically determined by the general public but *screened* by party primaries and caucuses, subsequently nominated at the National Party Conventions, and only then do they vie for the public vote. To be sure the President of the USA is *elected*, not however by the people at large but by an Electoral College comprising *appointed* Electors. The Vice President is simply *chosen* by the President and serves at his discretion. The President's Cabinet (The Executive Branch) and the Judicial Branch of government are *appointed* by the President with but the nominal consent of the Senate. Only the members of Congress are actually democratically elected and even their popular election is marred by the vast sums of money necessary for election campaigns.

The manner in which our government functions from top to bottom is no less flawed democratically than is its structure. Over the years, our Presidents have autocratically extended the considerable sweep of power accorded them by the Constitution. Presidential Executive Privilege has become tainted by rank abuse. Presidential practices that violate both the Constitution and the tenets of Democracy have become legion. George W. Bush is but the latest of our Presidents to declare war without the consent of Congress. In the name of national security, Bush's White House has made a mockery of civil rights: court warrants for house searches, for wiretapping and for the release of confidential information have become executively approved warrantless invasions of the constitutionally guaranteed privacy of private citizens. Human rights argued by Democracy and the Geneva Conventions, and protected by the Constitution have been no less cavalierly violated by presidential decree, and again in the name of security: Concern for America's safety was for Bush adequate justification for the secret commitment ("extraordinary renditions") of suspected enemy terrorists to such obliging countries as Poland, Rumania, Syria and Egypt for "enhanced interrogation" (torture)and for the secret and indefinite imprisonment and "enhanced interrogation" of so-called "enemy combatants" in Iraq (Abu Ghraib) and Cuba (Guantanamo). No less undemocratic than this flagrant breeching of civil and human rights is Bush's autocratic extension of his presidential right to veto bills to signed-letter line vetoes and his opportunistic overuse of his right to make unscrutinized government appointments when Congress is not in session. On the presidential plane, Democracy has clearly suffered a severe blow!

American Democracy on the congressional plane has fared little better. The two-senators-per-state structure of the Senate has made for drastically unequal popular representation and disproportional allotment of power to sparsely populated states. The representation of the states in the House of Representatives does accord with popular count but is badly marred by the sporadic reshaping of the political districts by state legislators to guarantee their personal re-election and to serve party purposes more than state interests. Furthermore, the legislative decisions of both Senators and Representatives are just as badly tainted by the plethora of special-interest and well-heeled lobbyists frequenting the Halls of Congress. Even America's stubbornly prevailing two-party political system has not been conducive to a sound Democracy: Party loyalty has too frequently taken precedence over national concerns and party bickering has too often peaked in legislative gridlock. Nor have the legal decisions of the appointed Judiciary been untouched by nominator and party allegiance.

Each of the three branches—executive, legislative and judicial—of America's government is plainly democratically wanting in a few or even in many ways. And for good reason! Both the governed many and the governing few have themselves been wanting in their democratic credentials. The many are too many and too heterogeneous, too poorly schooled in politics, too indifferent politically, too otherwise preoccupied, too accepting and too passive. And the privileged few, the wealthy, the more educated, the more enterprising and the politically more informed and more astute have been all too willing to compromise America's Democracy for wealth and power. What Americans got is what Americans wrought. The many and the few have also wrought an American culture that is no less responsible for America's flawed form of Democracy.

A culture that features radical individualism, unfettered capitalism, raw materialism, rank consumerism and blatant hedonism cannot but feature a diminished Democracy. Indeed, America's Democracy has become more autocratic and plutocratic than it is democratic.

Democracy is an idea, a sociopolitical ideal that in times past and present has sporadically become a reality, a reality that has always fallen short of its ideal. America's birthing of Democracy is but one of many such examples. America's Democracy is badly flawed, but so is every other present-day Democracy, and none of history's Democracies fared any better. Movement from noumenon to phenomenon inevitably results in imperfection and disillusionment. Neither should dissuade scrutiny to improve an idea's imperfect manifestation. And that is what America should be intent upon and not hell bent on exporting its flawed Democracy.

Our Financial Crisis

*T*hanks to its unfettered capitalism, America is in economic and political disarray. After months of politically motivated denial by the White House that the country is in a *recession*, we are suddenly threatened by an awful *depression*.

Chairman Ben Bernanke of the Federal Reserve and Henry Paulson, Secretary of the Treasury, together with President George W. Bush, are convinced that an immediate 700-million-dollar bailout of Wall Street and its financial institutions is necessary to avert a melt-down of the American economy. Disregarding the pleas of the leaders of both parties, an agitated House of Representatives has chosen to vote against the proposed remedy. More heated debate will now follow.

What is now essentially a Wall Street bailout will have to become a bill that at least appears to be of benefit to both Wall Street and Main Street. Both of these worlds, and not one or the other, have to be coddled to prevent a likely collapse of the financial arena and of the housing market. Congress will have to achieve a precarious balance in its legislation. To favor Wall Street would be to jeopardize the housing market and to favor the latter could leave Wall Street in disarray. May our solons make a wise decision! May they address the symptoms and not just the disease! Even if it is this that they do, the country's financial recovery is likely to take several or more years.

Unfettered capitalism—and this is the engine that drives America's economy—eventually burns to its own destruction. Perhaps we Americans have learned our lesson. A sensibly regulated and socially responsible capitalism promises greater stability and broader satisfaction.

Hope springs eternal!

Essayistic Ventures and Topical Asides

The Actual and the Virtual

*H*uman beings are essentially very inquisitive. We want to know what is going on in the world around us. In the Middle Ages and earlier, people focussed on and became intimately acquainted with their immediate environment—with the home, the village and very little more. This very confined area of experience expanded with the passing of the centuries and the progressively greater mobility of the common people. By the 20th century, and thanks to our ready modern modes of travel, the whole world and all its peoples had become common experience for most of the many. This general acquaintance with the actual world and its actual people peaked by the middle of the 20th century. Since then, with the spread of the television and advent of the computer, a virtual electronics world has in our experience gradually edged our old actual world aside. Today more and more people have begun to feel more and more at home in the virtual world that now envelops us than in the actual world in which we have our being.

In this regard progress spells regress!

Presidential Primaries, Caucuses, National Party Conventions and the Electoral College

Prologue

The road to the presidency is a long and tortuous experience for both voters and presidential candidates. The unsettling journey begins with a confusing quadrennial array of party primaries and caucuses that peak in national party conventions which, in turn, are followed by a general national election, and all finally culminates in the election of a president by The Electoral College.

Primaries, Caucuses and National Party conventions

Both national political parties have an initial dizzying prolonged flurry of primaries and caucuses—meetings of registered voters and gatherings of party activists—for the purpose of choosing delegates for their national conventions. Each state's allotment of presidential delegates is proportional to its population. For our present presidential election, the Democratic Convention numbered 3,253 delegates, and the Republican Convention, 2,380, and to these numbers, the former added 794 superdelegates and the latter, 123. In each case, the superdelegates are current or former office holders and party officials who represent the mainstream of their party's thought and policy: self-appointed party elders intent upon steering their conventions in their choice of presidential candidates.

National Elections and the Electoral College

The party conventions are customarily followed by five to six months of relentless presidential campaigning highlighted by debates of the presidential hopefuls. Campaigns and debates only rarely transcend simplistic politics and empty promises, are characterized by slogans, mantras, halftruths, opponent denigrations, all repeated *ad nauseam,* leave the average American more bewildered than informed and the informed thoughtful citizen frustrated and disillusioned. This, while the true believers of both parties shout their wild approval. And all ends in a national election and the popular approval but not election of one of the presidential candidates. The president is, in fact, elected by an Electoral College set up by the founders of America who were suspicious of pure Democracy. George W. Bush's second election to the presidency was the latest of three occasions when this built-in checkmating of real Democracy nullified the national popular vote.

Epilogue

Our present sixteen months of bedlam from the presidential election's preliminaries to its conclusion, is more than our founding fathers bargained for when they drew up the Constitution in 1787. The presidential election process has become a bewildering mess, a veritable circus driven by money, orchestrated by special interest groups and celebrated by the media. And all this ado has resulted in a two-party system that has literally disenfranchised all those of different political persuasion. It is high time for serious reflection and political reform!

America would do well to accommodate more political parties (e.g. Peace and Freedom Party, the Greens, Libertarians and the American Independents). A proportionally representative Democracy would be a decided improvement over our present limited representative Democracy. Our present presidential election's twenty-one months of scattered turmoil should be replaced by a disciplined maximum three-month campaign. And to make a democracy of our plutocracy, money must cease to be the engine that for all drives our elections and determines our legislation. Last but not least: the Electoral College—as has been recommended countless times over the years—should be eliminated. True Democracy demands a popularly elected president.

It is high time for serious reflection and political reform!

The Professional and the Amateur

*T*he few have since time immemorial been society's shakers, breakers and makers. Times are a-changing! The twilight of the Gods is approaching. Thanks to the Internet's democratizing of society, to its tapping of the crowd, to its empowerment of the relatively untutored and to its fostering of the cult of the amateur, the diminuation of the professionals is in the offing. The Internet has given power to anyone who chooses to exercise it, and an ever-increasing number of the "unwashed" is succumbing to that temptation. Bloggers by the droves are becoming citizen-journalists, gossip columnists, snake-oil salespeople, financial wizards, spiritual gurus, unorthodox economists, medical advisers, literary critics, art historians and soothsayers of whatever ilk. And since the Internet is interlinking everyone with everyone, whatever one seeks can readily be found, whatever one lacks is generously provided and whatever ails one is promptly treated. The best of all worlds appears to have dawned!

Unfortunately, this Internet miracle of the Electronics Age is anything by the Oracle of Delphi that its aficionados would have it be. Neither dispensing bloggers nor the inquisitive public at large are up to their challenges. The bloggers are by and large not adequately informed to inform and the Internet surfers are, as a whole, too unprepared and too undiscerning to capably vet the plethora of raw material at their disposal.

Enthusiastic bloggers and surfers have blinded themselves to reality. The virtual reality of the Electronics World is holding sway. Opinion, belief, half-truths and outright misinformation are having their populist heyday. This Internet give and take of the ordinary many has become an exhilarating preoccupation, a bubble of enthusiasm.

It was America's irrational exuberance that puffed up the financial bubble that burst in 2008. It is the same characteristically American irrational exuberance that spawned the Internet's populist bubble. Fortunately, this populist bubble, like all bubbles, is doomed to burst. It is only a matter of time before amateurs will again defer to professionals, and the general public will be the better served for it.

Language

Standard Language

Standard languages have always been buffetted by their colloquial counterparts. The words and expressions of everyday language are ever-changing in pronunciation and meaning and ever being discarded and replaced, and spoken language's syntax keeps evolving. These changes in the spoken language compel selective changes in the standard language. Though connected in their continuous flux, both languages have always gone their separate ways. A change in this traditional balanced parallel flow of languages appears to be in the offing. The radically changing social circumstances of our Electronics Age—thanks by and large to the Internet's burgeoning social networking—have begun to refashion our popular and standard languages. Now that everyone seems to be talking and texting with everyone else regardless of station in life and geographical location, an unprecedented levelling off of language is inevitable. The probable melding of the common and of the cultivated, promises a single language, a new standard language, a language that is more studied, more discerning and more expressive than today's rough and ready everyday language of the many, and less scholarly, less incisive and less elegant than today's elitist language of the few. An elevating and a lowering. A democratization of America's standard English!

Spoken Language

Americans have never been notably language conscious. Spoken language, in particular, has always been rather shoddy. Of late, American English, spoken both by the uncouth and the couth, has become deplorably sloppy. Trivial words and phrases are commonly used too frequently, and for no compelling reasons (e.g.: things, stuff; exactly, absolutely, certainly, really; in terms of, in respect to, with regard to, from the standpoint of, you know, as it were, there you are, you understand) and very ordinary words are regularly misused for reasons of ignorance (e.g.: less and fewer, amount and number, most and majority). Grammar has fared no better (e.g.: me for I, was for were, who for whom, which for that, there is for there are, loan for lend, lay for lie). This hackneyed and imprecise language is being spread far and wide by the Internet's ever growing number of social networking sites (e.g.: Myspace, Facebook, Twitter) and is, in the extremes of the process, being reduced to telegrammic tweets. And this dismembering of the spoken language is being hastened in no small way by the very popular shorthand texting of the ubiquitous cell phone.

How long will it be before America's written English follows suit?

Figurative Language

Figurative language is only imprecisely informative and only vaguely elucidative. On the other hand, it is aesthetically pleasing, appeal as it does more to the imagination and emotions than to reason and logic. It is inherently a literary language! In fields other than literature, figurative language is attractive verbal dressing when used in moderation, and when used in excess, it becomes serious distraction. Discreet use of figurative language is a *sine qua non!*

Obscene Language

Obscenities, profanities and swear words of whatever ilk and mild or deeply offensive, are on the tip of almost everybody's tongue. Every language has its fair share of this asocial mode of verbal expression. Some languages, among them Hungarian and Rumanian, are blessed/cursed with an appalling abundance of shocking defamations. American English, French and Spanish have their fair share of colorful vulgar speech. German, Danish and Norwegian, on the other hand, seem to suffer a distinct dearth of catchy taboo language. In all these instances, vulgar language focusses primarily on the illicit, particularly on sex, sexual organs and excrement, and is expressly intent upon insult and humiliation. The immediate satisfaction and relief that a discharge of obscenity affords its purveyor is, of course, more than offset by the rancor and ill will left in its wake.

Obscene language dehumanizes both abuser and victim. It is clearly best avoided.

Addendum:

It is interesting to note that in Hungary's and Rumania's once numerous German-speaking communities dating back to the eighteenth century, the paucity of outrageous obscenities in their native tongue induced the Germans to commonly give expression to their bile in Hungarian and/or in Rumanian. An exchange of vile sentiment in a foreign tongue is, of course, a far more innocuous and less forbidding experience for both curser and cursed than the same exchange in a native language—a sort of swearing and being sworn at without actually swearing and being sworn at.

Cause for Pause

The Internet is encroaching upon the territory of the newspaper world, and that is so, not because it is a good thing, but because it has become possible and because it is an exhilarating novelty. Everyone who so chooses can gossip, report or voice his/her opinion at will, at any time and at any place. MySpace, Facebook, Twitter *et alia* are at everyone's disposal. Everyone can join the chorus regardless of voice or ear!

Needless to say, the result has been a deafening cacophony of undigested and unvetted fragmented information, misinformation, disinformation and hearsay. And this chaotic medium promises to antiquate our once ubiquitous and treasured newspapers.

Money is the determinant in this questionable process. Advertisers and their dollars are following the throng to the Internet, steadily reducing newspaper revenues and, in turn, the cadres of professional reporters and commentators, newspaper coverage and circulation. In due time, this transformation is likely to force most newspapers out of business.

This mass participation in newscasting has had immediate mass appeal. The general public has thronged to the Internet for the latest about anything. Should this persist, America will eventually lose a vital far-reaching educational institution and an indispensable treasure trove of socio-political information for historians.

The floundering ship may yet right itself before it founders!

Addendum:

May our paperbook, too, eventually give way to a primarily electronically available facsimile?

More cause for pause!

Economic Authoritarianism

Economic authoritarianism, alias financial-world dictatorship, prevails in America.

America's financial world is answerable to no one. In the course of the past fifty odd years, our government gradually became little more than an obsequious handmaiden to this monstrous monetary engine and our courts gradually slipped into its shadow, and Americans, all along, remained by and large too otherwise preoccupied to become alarmed by this violation of their treasured democracy.

It was only of late, when our latest financial bubble burst, that eyes suddenly opened to the ugly reality that America had become.

That President Obama's Whitehouse will succeed in dismantling plutocratic America and in resurrecting democratic America is anything but certain.

An Armageddon awaits us!

America's Foreign Debt

America's foreign debt looms large at home and ever larger abroad. If not checked, the present rapid growth of this burden promises, sooner or later, to topple America from its top-dog international dais. Measures to preclude this possibility could and should be taken by President Obama's Whitehouse, and as soon as possible.

A draconian across-the-board cut in government spending is imperative.

An income-tax reform that will place a heavier financial burden upon the shoulders of America's wealthy is equally imperative.

A progressive consumption sales tax is long overdue.

Measures such as these could gradually reduce America's financial dependence upon China and Japan, could eventually shrink the foreign debt to a non-threatening size and could leave America an enviable world power both politically and economically.

We shall see!

Private Enterprise

*M*inimally-fettered private enterprise has for the past four decades been the engine that drives America's capitalist economy. Free-ranging private enterprise's causative role in the recent boom and bust of America's financial world has become obvious, its negative impact upon other essential national services is only beginning to cause alarm. Particularly in question are America's medical care, its postal service and its educational system.

America's fractured medical-care system has long been the private fiefdom of the insurance and pharmaceutical industries. For these two hardnosed private services, America's wellbeing has been a veritable treasure trove. America's medical costs per capita are the highest in the world while its medical care is only mid-range compared with that of other major Western industrialized nations. That medical care and prescription drugs are beyond the financial reach of some 45 million Americans is unacceptable. Private enterprise has had its questionable fling in the field of medical care and it is high time that America—as all other Western industrialized countries did years ago—give nationalized medical care an opportunity to prove itself.

It was not until well on in the second half of the last century that private enterprise for profit began to gnaw away at America's nationalized postal system and public education. Private companies, among them, UPS (its national service began in 1977) and FedEx (1978), began to stake out and exploit lucrative postal services, The service provided by these private operations, albeit good, has unfortunately not been without broad untoward consequences. Private enterprise's gainful intrusion was tantamount to a financial undermining of the U.S. Postal Service that resulted in a general curtailment of and decline in its many services. Gain in special delivery has been more than offset by loss in general delivery.

The U.S. Postal Service was anything but a model of efficiency long before the intrusion of UPS in 1977. Reform had long been in order. Unfortunately partial privatization only added to the department's woes. Internal rather than external reform would undoubtedly have served America better.

Private enterprise's venture into the field of America's national public education has been even more questionable than its foraging in the mail world. There is obviously a place for both private and public schools. Both serve their specific purposes and America would be the better for it if both were to remain intact and healthy. While traditional private schools are faring reasonably well, public schools have been questioned and under attack for decades. This has spawned a veritable invasion of the public school educational system by zealous private enterprise for profit. With promises of a superior and cost-effective education, organizations such as the for-profit Edison Schools (1922–) quickly spread across the country. Unfortunately, private enterprise's fervent promises of better educational possibility has proved to be more rhetoric than reality and the public school world has been left more undermined and demoralized than duly instructed. Necessary educational reform might better have been internal rather than intrusive.

Matters of critical national concern should obviously be administered nationally and for the commonweal and not run privately for profit. America's medical care should never have been allowed to slip into the hands of private enterprise for profit, and care should be taken that its postal service and education do not suffer the same fate. A privatization of America's national defense would rightly raise a hue and cry!

It must be remembered that in America private enterprise is decidedly more committed to monetary return than to excellence.

Our Nuclear World

At the outset of July 2009, America and Russia, the world's two major powerhouses held yet another summit meeting to grapple anew with the scourge of our modern era—nuclear weapons!

Our nuclear world was ushered in with deadly fanfare when America, in August of 1945, dumped an atom bomb on Japan's

Hiroshima, and then another, a few days later, on Nagasaki. Both cities were obliterated and the death toll was appalling. Russia tested its first nuclear warhead in 1949, America countered with a hydrogen bomb in 1951, and Russia responded with its H-bomb in 1953. The cold-war nuclear arms race was off with a bang!

By the end of the 20th century, in mutual fear and in deadly competition for world supremacy, America and Russia had together stockpiled some 20,000 nuclear weapons, enough to blow up the world a hundred times over. By then, too, France, England, Israel, India, Pakistan and China had joined the nuclear club, and a number of other countries, among them, Libya, North Korea and Iran, were aspiring to do so. Nuclear proliferation was threatening to get out of hand!

After the break-up of the Russian empire in 1991, anti-Americanism in Russia and anti-Russianism in America subsided briefly in official circles. The nuclear cache of each country was to be reduced and anti-missile tests were to be halted. Signed agreements between America and Russia proved to be token, nuclear arsenals were only slightly reduced and missile, and anti-missile testing was only briefly interrupted. By the turn of the century, mutual antipathy was back to its level of the cold-war years, both countries began again to augment their weapons of mass destruction, and each country resumed its military and political checkmating of the other.

When President G.W. Bush began his aggressive containment of Russia—America's sponsorship of NATO's eastward expansion, its plans to locate anti-ballistic missile stations in Poland and in the Czech Republic, its alliance with the anti-Russian faction in the Ukraine, its army bases and airfields located in Rumania, Georgia, Kazakhstan, Tajikistan *et al.*, and America's support of Georgia in its war with Russia—it predictably elicited a Russian promise of reciprocal, and if necessary, nuclear response. This was the awful kettle of fish that President Obama inherited in January of 2009, and it was to defuse this explosive situation that he and President Medvedev of Russia held their summit meeting in July of 2009.

Was the summit meeting fruitful, and if so, to what extent? This remains to be seen. The meeting was allegedly more reserved than friendly and fortunately more pragmatic than ideological. Unfortunately, only common interests were addressed and serious differences were put aside for a future summit. Of major importance was a preliminary agreement to limit the deployed arsenal of each country to 1500 warheads. The door was also left open for a further reduction of warheads in a new Strategic Reduction Treaty that could follow by the end of 2009. That all this could one day lead to a world free of nuclear weapons is as yet more pipe dream than likelihood. In the meantime, the Comprehensive Test Ban Treaty of 1994 has yet to be signed by America, the Nuclear Non-Proliferation Treaty of 1968 has to be strengthened by more comprehensive inspections and more severe penalties for violators, higher security has to be provided for the world's vulnerable nuclear materials, and deployed nuclear weapons should be removed from high alert to reduce the risk of accidental launch.

Much between America and Russia has still to be negotiated and settled. Nevertheless, the Obama/Medvedev summit may have set the world on a new and more promising course than past summits.

If the powers that be do not manage to mend fences and are unable to control and eventually to eliminate nuclear weapons, these weapons will continue to control and may eventually eliminate mankind.

A Moral Crisis and Beyond

*A*merica is not experiencing a *financial crisis*. To be more precise, it is suffering from dire financial woes, and these derive from a *crisis of values*.

Embraced values are the guidelines that determine the sundry paths a society takes, be they in domestic policies or foreign affairs. Money, material things and power have become America's major passions and almost any means necessary to achieve these ends has become quite acceptable. The esteem that traditional Christian-Judaic values have continued to enjoy, has in fact become little more than lip service. Nor is America, in this regard, an exception among the industrialized nations of the Western World.

Power-besot America's invasion of Iraq, its financial world's licentious scramble for wealth, Mr. and Mrs. America's ready complicity with this money-lending realm, and America's wanting medical care monopolized by profiteering insurance companies, its financially neglected public education and its shoddy treatment and exploitation of its millions of legal and illegal immigrants are but a few of the most egregious examples of America's moral French leave. Passion for power, avarice and grandee mentality had become America's springboard of policy and practice. Traditional moral restraint was obviously for the birds!

We Americans have permitted ourselves to do freely and brazenly and seldomly with any moral compunctions what was once only done more rarely and clandestinely and with, more often than not, a troubled conscience. It is to this moral shift that America owes most of its present woes. It is no less this drift that accounts for America's present response to these many woes. Ends are again paramount and morality is again more shelved than not. This certainly does not augur well. More of the same questionable approach is only likely to trail more of the same questionable results.

To preclude a repetition of repetitions, America's empire mindedness, casino capitalism, radical individualism, raw materialism and avid consumerism clearly have to be curtailed and moderated by an intact system of sound moral values. But is this return to a remote past still possible, or has our Western Christian-Judaic culture in its decline already reached its stage of no return? If indeed, as has been argued, ours is an age of cultural twilight, then nothing new can be expected until the seeds of a new culture are sown, sprout and spread. It is probably the birth of something new and not a rejuvenation of the old that lies in store for us.

Let's buckle up. A rough ride awaits us!

News

The publication of news in America is in the throes of a radical change. Newspapers are shrinking and disappearing, professional reporters and commentators are dwindling in their numbers and news is becoming threadbare and repetitive. The concerned older generation, to whom the reading of a newspaper became a daily ritual, is lamenting this decline, while the unperturbed electronics-age generation is given wholeheartedly to the Internet's popular dissemination of news.

Any radical change in the manner in which news is received will inevitably mean a painful change in reading habit but it can also, in recompense, improve news coverage and reliability. To date, unfortunately, this transition from printed news to electronically delivered news has done little more than make a mockery of the news world. Traditional responsible professional reportage is giving way to the unvetted splintered information of the Internet's everyman, and traditional informed political, social and cultural commentary is becoming spotty chance comment.

The old is dying and the new is still in its infant stage. In due time our traditional newspaper will likely become a thing of the past, and in due time, our present very wanting electronically disseminated news and commentary are likely to become as professional as the news and commentary of the traditional newspaper. If such is the case, nothing will have changed in the world of news but for the manner of delivery and the habit of reading.

Xenophobia II

The other, the stranger, the foreigner has always been a cause for serious concern, just as one's own, the known have always been a comfortable haven.

The unknown is suspect, it perplexes, disturbs, annoys, angers, poses a threat and rouses fear and hostility. Fear of the stranger has always led to flight and safety and anger and hostility have generally ended in the defeat or victory of ugly battle. These *flight* or *fight* responses are reflexive and natural survival-driven impulses that have served their purposes for millennia. Both reactions are still current and still serve their ultimately questionable and provisional objectives: to escape or to nullify the foreigner.

As the human community slowly evolved from isolated nomadic tribes to fixed bordering nations a desirable alternative to *flight* or *fight* gradually surfaced. Intermingling, interaction, co-dependence and growing mutual understanding began to reduce suspicion, fear and hostility. The present incipient globalization of the world's nations, the ever-greater intermingling of its racial and ethnic groups, promises in due time to seriously attenuate, if not to end, one of mankind's oldest afflictions: xenophobia.

A real possibility or a pious hope?

To Forgive

What is it to forgive? What is it that forgiveness does? Nothing untoward said or done can ever be unsaid or undone by forgiveness, nor for that matter by punishment or excuse. These different responses only deal judgmentally with transgression and do not in any way alter or wipe it out. What has been said or done cannot be retracted, but the different reactions can make more or less of the offense and can resolve it more or less favorably.

When excused, offenders are content but the offended are left somewhat disquieted. Duly punished, offenders are left incensed and the offended rather satisfied. In contrast to these conflicting results, when forgiveness prevails, both offenders and offended feel the better for it.

Excuse tends to treat transgression indulgently. Punishment is rarely remedial. Forgiveness promises better things to come.

Christianity was both psychologically astute and practical when it made forgiveness one of its prevailing tenets!

In contrast, Judaism's "eye for an eye and tooth for a tooth" had only left embittered and vengeful impaired in its wake.

Online Education

Ours is the dawn of online education. Actual schools with classrooms, teachers, books, desks and chalkboards may in the not-too-distant future become things of the past. Instead of classroom instruction and discussion, students with laptops will chat online with teachers and fellow students and get all study materials from the Web.

Aficionados of the electronic education promise a more efficient and more effective education than our present wanting schools offer. To be sure, violent campuses, overcrowded classrooms and rowdy hallways will not plague the new virtual school and less real estate and fewer teachers will be necessary, but online education demands a measure of self-discipline beyond most schoolchildren, lack of socialization and physical exercise will be seriously damaging to growing children, and the promised academic improvement is little more than pie in the sky.

That our present school system could do with some improvement goes without saying. That it is in need of a wholesale replacement is a very questionable contention.

America's Public Schools

A country is what its schools turn out. America's prominence both in the sciences and the arts does credit to its variety and abundance of first-class universities. While these institutions have over the years been esteemed and lavished with praise, America's secondary and elementary schools have never enjoyed much respect and have long been a favorite target of bitter criticism. Much of this ill-will has been directed at the teachers of these schools and most of it has been unwarranted and counterproductive.

The general public's low esteem for public-school teachers is clearly reflected in the low salaries accorded them. Low salaries in America reflect low status, in this case lower than that of registered nurses, certified accountants or even plumbers. Given this lack of esteem and low financial reward, it is surprising that the teaching profession has continued to attract a respectable number of highly qualified and very dedicated professionals. Yes, the profession does harbor its fair share of inadequates and misfits, but their number is relatively small. Unfortunately, these less than adequate teachers have attracted more adverse criticism than their small number deserves, and at the expense of their qualified colleagues. An irate public has simply concluded that all or most teachers are an inept lot ever in need of close administrative supervision, of repeated refresher courses and of constant counselling and guidance. Rather than allow teachers to become enterprising, to use their imaginations, to tap their own resourcefulness and to determine for themselves what is pedagogically best for their students, the powers that be—and with the full concurrence of the public—have simply imposed teaching methods prescribed by non-teaching teaching experts. The results have been less than satisfactory, and to no informed thoughtful person's surprise. Teachers have been demoralized, students have been shortchanged, administrators have been left confounded and parents have become vocally discontent.

A drastic change is clearly in order, or better, long overdue. Public-school teachers should obviously be accorded the respect due all socially important professions, and their salaries should be commensurate. Respectable status and fair remuneration will do much to draw more of our better college graduates into the profession than is now the case. But this of itself will not be enough to turn the tide. Working conditions must also change drastically. Education, now a political toy and the fief of professional administrators, has to be put into the hands of teachers and principals. These professionals, now menials, should be given the authority they deserve and the accordant responsibility. The present pedagogic bits must be removed and reins must be loosened. The initiative, imagination and resourcefulness of dedicated teachers must be allowed the free play they are now denied. Teachers will rise to the occasion if permitted to do so!

But still more change is necessary. For maximal educational benefit, the number of students in a given class should be adjusted to accommodate the subject and the grade. That classes may not exceed a given number of students—as is now the mandate—is good but does not go far enough. A more sophisticated approach to numbers is necessary. Furthermore, classrooms should be more adequate in size and more appropriately equipped for their purposes than now is generally the case. Necessary school supplies should also not have to depend upon the financial generosity of the teacher, as too is now all too often the case.

Things are clearly not what they could or should be in our public schools. Too much has gone awry educationally, efforts to remedy matters have been wrong-headed and the results dismal. And primarily to blame teachers for our schools' educational failures—a practice to which the general public and educational bureaucrats have become quite accustomed—is seriously myopic. The entire educational system is geared for something less than success. For this, our schools of education, school administrators, the politicians who vote school monies and the general public, all share blame with the teachers. And a dyed-in-the wool American anti-intellectualism lurks behind it all.

An addendum is in order. Educational success depends upon three and not just one institution. The first of these is the family school, the second is the public school and the third is the social school. If parents opt to do their share, if teachers are allowed to do their share and if society is prepared to provide the necessary moral and financial support, matters educational would improve dramatically. Education is a shared responsibility!

Spelling

The spelling of English has always bewildered schoolchildren and has never ceased to perplex and vex adults.

Too many vowel-consonant clusters have different pronunciations (e.g. though, thought, slough, through; sew, few, lewd), too many similarly pronounced vowel/consonant are spelled differently (e.g. ought, slaughter; loot, suit; feel, heal), and vowels have too often been reduced to a schwa while retaining their identity in spelling (e.g. forcible, tolerable; leader, monitor; instance, insistence; defendant, repellent).

These are but a few of the plethora of daunting challenges of current English spelling.

A periodic spelling reform to keep spelling reasonably abreast of pronunciation is definitely in order.

Why continue to endure an unnecessary time-consuming irritation?

Food

We are doomed if we have too little and doomed if we have too much!

Over the years, millions of people in the third-world countries have starved for want of sufficient food. In the industrialized world and particularly in the USA, thousands upon thousands of people die annually for their excessive consumption of food.

Since the world produces ample food to feel all of its peoples, the problem that plagues poor countries could be solved by a fairer distribution of the plentiful available food. The world's health is at stake!

How long will it be before the haves share their plenty with the havenots?

America's problem is both simpler and more complex than that of the world's poor countries. Americans are victims of America's plentitude of almost everything and particularly of its abundance of inexpensive food. Americans are also the willing victims of America's food industry's pervasive appetizing advertising. Resultantly, junk-food, and in particular fastfoods, has become a ubiquitous obsession. Indeed, fastfoods have become a general addiction and Americans are suffering the inevitable consequences.

Widespread obesity sparing no age groups has begun to take its health toll in America: diabetes, both type one and two, is becoming commonplace; cholesterol counts and blood pressures have become deplorably high; and heart attacks and strokes have increased alarmingly. America is approaching a health crisis!

Eating habits can be deeply entrenched and appetite, once whetted, is hard to curb. Consequently, to modify America's eating for the better will require serious action on at least two fronts: America's food industry must willynilly begin to focus more on healthy foods than on hefty profits and Americans will have to learn how to eat more discreetly and more moderately. More readily available sound nutritional information and less seductive advertising would help matters.

When, if ever, will America go this route?

As long as the world's plentiful food is not distributed more equitably, too many people in its poor countries will continue to starve to death, and just as long as Americans do not change their eating habits, too many of them will continue to eat themselves to death!

When will humanity, reason and common sense begin to prevail?

Water

Oil, once plentiful, has become a rare commodity that unfortunately determines both America's well-being and America's foreign policy.

Potable water, no longer as plentiful as it once was, will become a matter of major concern—another irksome commodity—in the not too distant future. An inadequate supply of water will be just as devastating and as compelling as has been the dwindling supply of oil. To preclude this possibility, vigorous and wise measures will soon have to be enacted.

To conserve water, its recycling will be imperative. The resultant "grey water" will do for the watering of lawns and gardens, the washing down of driveways and the flushing of toilets. California's huge and heavily-irrigated desert farms will also have to be phased out. And to supplement the dwindling supply of potable water, costly desalination plants will soon have to dot the coastlines of America. Eventually too, a grey-water plumbing system will have to be added to the present plumbing of every house and every building.

Drastic and expensive innovations have always attracted loud popular objections. This notwithstanding, the sooner all or just some of the above-mentioned measures are enacted, the better.

A stitch in time saves nine!

A Perverse Proclivity

*A*merica is swimming in money!

There was money galore to bail out America's troubled financial institutions.

The insurance, pharmaceutical and oil industries, together with America's financial world, have enough greenbacks to reward their CEO's with astronomical salaries and lush bonuses, and still have enough left over to keep their shareholders more than happy.

And vast sums of money are always available for America's wars, billions of dollars are annually allotted, and for questionable purposes, to such disparate countries as Pakistan, Israel and Columbia, and financially strapped countries such as Poland, Rumania, Czechoslovakia and Georgia have been liberally bribed financially to do America's bidding. Yet, despite this extravagance, there has been a chronic dearth of money for improving America's wanting public schools, little money to spare for a long overdue overhaul of America's inadequate system of healthcare, even less money available for wiping out America's disgracefully widespread poverty, and no money, to date, for urgently needed climate control.

America is extravagant when it might better be tightfisted and tightfisted when it might better be extravagant.

Abominable choices and wretched consequences!

From Surge to Plunge

*I*f America's Financial Services Industry is not to continue to experience its unsettling periodic bubbles and busts, it will have to be drastically reformed and strictly regulated. It has become more than obvious that the financial world, left to its own devices, will gamble recklessly for its own advantage and regardless of any resultant risk for the country as a whole.

While a financial bubble endures, the wealthy few become even wealthier and the ordinary many enjoy a brief pseudo prosperity, and when the bubble bursts the wealthy few lose some of their wealth while too many of the ordinary many are left jobless and homeless. Financial bubbles and bursts take a country economically from extreme to extreme and leave its citizens emotionally in a constant state of turmoil.

To assume that America's financial world will ever be informed, thoughtful and humane enough to modify its hard-nosed risk-taking money-making practices enough to prevent the money market's euphoric surges and devastating plunges, is more pious hope than realistic expectation, human nature being what it is. It is amply clear that a self-regulated financial world's unfettered capitalism must become less self-serving and more socially responsible, both for its own benefit and America's financial stability.

America's banks and its sundry financial institutions should not be allowed to grow too large to fail, banks should be restricted to traditional banking, and the financial world's business practices will have to be closely regulated by government agencies with some real clout. The likelihood that a Congress paralyzed by party politics and highly beholden to the financial world will ever pass the legislation necessary for such a restructuring and regulation is highly doubtful.

The Financial Services Industry is much more likely legislatively to suffer no more than minor modifications and restrictions and to continue willfully to take America from surge to plunge and back again.

Such is also likely to be the unfortunate lot of America's wanting healthcare. It, too, will continue to lumber along its capricious course with but minor Band-Aid changes, and in this case, thanks to the financial clout of the insurance world and of the pharmaceutical industry, and to the paralysis of Congress.

A Clash of Empires

*T*wo empires are on a collision course: *Imperium Americanum,* the world's dominant power for the past sixty years, and successor-minded imperial China.

China has, or will soon have its own vision of a better world. What this vision is or will be promises to be of paramount importance to the USA, indeed to the whole world. World peace and prosperity could be in the offing or another Cold War with its world-wide negative repercussions could be on the threshold. Should America and China become bitter adversaries, the latter could take place and if their respective visions of a better world are reconcilable and their foreign policies are not at variance, the former could be the result.

Unlike America's Cold War with a declining Russia, a similar confrontation with a modernized and much more potent China would undoubtedly end disastrously for the USA. America could become the relatively impotent power that Russia became in its confrontation with a more vibrant and resourceful rival.

Hopefully, wise heads will prevail in both camps. Power can be shared to mutual advantage, and the world would enjoy peace and prosperity.

America's Spent Well-Being
An Empire in the Making

Some fifty-five years ago, a prescient President Dwight Eisenhower warned America that its military-industrial complex could lead the nation down the garden path. The unholy alliance did just that, leaving behind an unbroken trail of ill-advised wars, invasions, occupations and military interferences in foreign wars:

Vietnam (1961–75), Persian Gulf War (1990–91),

Afghanistan (2001–), Iraq (2003–), Libya (1981 and 1986),

Grenada 1983, Haiti (1994–5), Kosovo (1999),

Salvadoran Civil War (1977–92), Honduran Guerrilla War (1981–90),

Lebanese Civil War (1982–84), Nicaraguan Civil War (1982–90),

Bosnian Civil War (1994–95).

The Pentagon had its military flings, the arms industry reaped its bounteous profits, and while American expansionism was well-served, America itself was left the worst for it, a country in moral, political and economic disarray.

This nefarious military adventurism of the military-industrial complex met little opposition. An empire-minded White House and Congress condoned and abetted it, and popular opposition was but spotty and weak.

Had Eisenhower been heeded, America's well-being might well have been spared!

Privacy under Assault

Not quite a decade ago, America's well-being began to be further seriously assaulted, and again by an unholy alliance, this time by a government and corporate complex. Following the devastating terrorist attack of September 11, 2001, disturbed by America's vulnerability, obsessed by a need for greater security and bolstered by a newly enacted Patriot bill, Washington's fledgling National Security Agency began a nationwide obnoxious snooping, a brazen invasion of personal and organizational privacy. Widespread clandestine surveillance of individuals and organizations, profuse wire-tapping and scrutinizing of e-mail without due authorization, indiscriminate stalking and apprehension of suspected terrorists, would-be terrorists and of ordinary individuals whether citizens or foreigners, and all too many illegal entry-and-search invasions of private homes, offices and mosques have made treasured traditional American privacy a thing of the past. Privacy became a dispensable inconvenience!

In its amoral business practices, the corporate world has of late been compromising America's privacy no less insidiously than the government. Customer information has become a treasure-trove for businesses of whatever ilk. This personal information is gathered surreptitiously, used for business advantage and increased profits and sold to yet other businesses and further profitable invasion of privacy. To make matters even worse, major corporations have been persuaded or coerced to share their proprietary information with the government, a further diminution of privacy, for the sake of America's security.

This almost conspiratorial evisceration of privacy by government and corporate world—a further blighting of America's well-being—has been made possible by the ingenious gadgetry of the electronics age and by the disturbing ignorance, appalling indifference and general lethargy of Americans as a whole. The blame is widespread!

Aftermath and Afterthought

Given this long-time and financially burdensome bellicose foreign policy and this egregious and widespread violation of civil rights of its more recent domestic policy, it was a foregone conclusion that America would become an international ogre and that America's general well-being would suffer a shocking deterioration. The full impact has yet to be felt!

Where are today's guardians of America's well-being and would they be heeded any more than was President Eisenhower?

America's spent well-being—
Too high a price
For empire dream,
Questionable security,
Bloody money!

Joseph Mileck   73

Genius

Genius—not high intelligence ability measured by performance or a standardized intelligence test, nor talent referring to unusual native aptitude for some special kind of work, but original creativeness—is a phenomenon that has intrigued the best and worst of minds for more than the past two thousand years.

Theories regarding the source and nature of genius have ranged from the sublime to the ridiculous. For some it has been nothing less than a God-given gift. Others have argued that genius simply belongs to a separate psychological species. Still others have associated it closely with drug and alcohol addiction. Yet others have disposed of it as a functional disorder of mind and emotions. And at the end of the 19th century, thanks largely to the eminent Italian criminologist Cesare Lombroso and to the prominent Zionist Max Nordau, genius and insanity became virtually one and the same. Nor was this shocker an entirely original theory. It echoed a conviction to which Lucius Seneca gave expression in the first century A.D.: "There is no great genius without some touch of madness."

Over the centuries following Seneca, many other worthies have commented on the source and nature of genius and no less candidly, eg.:

John Dryden: "Genius must be born, and never can be taught." (1693)

Elizabeth Barrett Browning (1806–1861): "Since when was genius found respectable?"

William James: "Genius . . . means little more than the faculty of perceiving in an unhabitual manner. (1890)

Thomas Edison: "Genius is one percent inspiration and ninety-nine percent perspiration." (1932)

Alone, each of the above capsule views of genius leaves too much unsaid. It is only when these pronunciamentos are refined and integrated with the help of today's leading neurobiologists (e.g. Nobelist Eric Kandel) that an acceptable if not final theory regarding the source and nature of genius begins to emerge, to wit:

Essayistic Ventures and Topical Asides

A genius is exceptional: is different and does things differently; is a rare originally creative deviation from the norm. It all begins with a not fully developed or early injured part of the brain and a compensatory overdevelopment of another part of the brain. Nurture then joins nature in a very fruitful conspiracy and the blighted become the blest: most frequently our musical, mathematical and recall geniuses.

The short of the long: Genius is primarily an unfortunate minus that fortuitously becomes a wondrous plus, the end result of a fertile interplay of compensatory nature and favorable nurture.

Addictions, neuroses, illnesses of whatever ilk and insanity are all but chance concomitant partner effects that color but do not spawn genius.

Creativity

*T*raditionally creativity was commonly deemed a wondrous God-given gift or but a chance unique talent. These yesteryear assumptions prevailed until the advent of modern-day psychology. With Freud, attention began to shift from these suspect sources of creativity to the very complex psychology of creativity. The road from creative potentiality to the creative process now became progressively more intricately psychological.

Creative potentiality (necessary intelligence and imagination) can vary dramatically from person to person. A modicum of inherent possibility to create demands a good deal of effort for fruition, an abundance correspondingly less. To wit, some trying honing—sweat and grief—is always necessary if potentiality is to become a creative skill. Creative potential would lie fallow but for some compelling motivation. Need and want seem to be the major motivating thrust in every kind of creativity: a need to counter the pain of wanting self-esteem and/or of the low regard of others, and a desire to raise low self-regard and/or the low regard of others. Creativity can therefore serve multiple purposes and can be twice rewarding: a blessing for the creator and a gratuitous gift for the public.

Creativity is thus essentially a catharsis, a wondrous therapeutic exercise, and this is true both of the genial and of the run-of-the-mill creators. Unfortunately, most blighted and blessed creative individuals are compelled to return to the well again and again for the psychological benefits of creativity are more or less short-lived.

The creative process itself is no pleasant saunter in a groomed grove, but an arduous crawl through taxing jungle thickets: torment that may end with a blissful *heurēka*.

Controversy and Violence

Violence has always been the individual's most ready response to controversy of whatever ilk. This is instinctive reflex response, basically animal-world protective and survival reaction. Such instinctive response may have been necessary, and therefore appropriate, for our ancestral cave dwellers, but is surely out of place in a civilized world. Today, most controversy between individuals does not pose a danger to life and limb and is therefore most appropriately resolved tranquilly and not violently. Unfortunately, violence between individuals has continued to flourish and, of course, continues only to breed new violence.

Wars—violence on a national scale—have always been and are likely to remain the characteristic response of countries to controversy. Defense and survival are again, rightly and mostly wrongly, considered adequate justification for violence. And wars, like violence between individuals, only breed new controversy and new violence.

Perhaps defense and survival have only been excuses for violence, or but secondary motivation for violence both on the plane of individuals and on the plane of nations. Perhaps mankind has always suffered from an intrinsic pathological attraction to, and an intrinsic delight and satisfaction in violence. If so, violence of whatever sort will continue *ad infinitum*.

Essayistic Ventures and Topical Asides

Post Scriptum:

Both thrusts are probably together responsible for mankind's proclivity for violence. Primal response to controversy and a pathological attraction to violence became a widespread perversity astounding and disheartening in its tenacity.

Thanks to this perversity, mankind, the most creative of all living things, also became the most destructive of all living things.

Representative Government

James Madison, fourth president of the United States (1809–1817), was persuaded that, in a Representative Democracy, it was the responsibility of the people to elect its representatives and the responsibility of the elected representatives to govern: "The genius of representative government comes from excluding the people in their collective capacity from the direct business of governing." Good governance, according to Madison, was clearly contingent upon a separation of functions. There are those who elect and there are those who govern.

Had President Madison over the years periodically returned from the dead to view the American scene, he would certainly have been appalled by the contrary evolution of American politics. Over the past 200 years, the electorate has become ever more intrusive in the governance of the country: the elected representatives have become ever more hectored by and ever more committed to the wishes of their particular constituencies. Particularism rapidly supplanted the commonweal and elected representatives became wily politicians more intent upon re-election than upon good governance.

This intrusion of the electorate into the "business of governing" culminated in the unabashed co-opting of governance by America's corporate world. Too many members of today's Congress owe their election to the financial support of powerful special interest groups, and too many of these alleged "representatives of the people" are in their governance very mindful of the legislative wishes of their financial backers. President Madison could not have imagined this possibility even in the worst of nightmares.

The America that was once something of a Representative Democracy has become something of a Representative Plutocracy. We've come a long way, baby.

President Madison must be having fits of exasperation in his grave!

Diplomacy

*D*iplomacy is an art that America has yet to master. To be mastered it has to be practised and for Americans there has never been sufficient pressing need to hone this skill. According to the strong, diplomacy is for the weak, and America has been the strongest among the strong for the past century.

For America's political leaders, diplomacy became a one-way American street what seems like ages ago. Unilateralism became America's international way of life. My way or the highway became the by-line of America's diplomatic language, and club or carrot became its persuaders. Thanks to its enormous financial resources, carrots have been plentiful in supply, and thanks to its military might—second to none in the world—the club has been large enough to intimidate all and sundry.

Such has been America's privileged role in international affairs. But times have changed, as is fortunately or unfortunately wont to be the case. Overreach since the Second World War has taken its toll. America's imperialism is dimming and dark clouds are forming on the Eastern horizon. The long threatened are becoming America's threateners.

But it may not yet be too late to learn and practise the old art of diplomacy.

Hope burns eternal!

Rebellion and Intervention

Widespread turmoil in the Arab world is in the foreground of a global socio-political awakening, an upheaval that portends foreign intervention. Countries intent upon exploitation, as well as countries anxious to be of assistance, are sorely tempted to intervene militarily.

Unfortunately, foreign intervention of whatever ilk only tends to add fuel to fire. Self-interest intervention, and even humanitarian military involvement intent solely upon stemming the mass killing of civilians by the warring factions, tend only to spawn new animosities, to prolong the socio-political chaos and to add to the slaughter and destruction.

The exploiting countries that intervene militarily should be severely censured by the United Nations and their membership in the organization revoked until due reparations have been made. For their military intervention, well-intentioned but misguided countries should be called to account in no uncertain terms, ordered to make reparations and to confine any future interventions to peaceful strategy. Any foreign military intervention should be limited to a temporary occupation of the fractured country by an effective force of peace-keeping soldiers under the auspices of the United Nations.

Wars, civil or between nations, have in themselves never settled anything for the better. Change for the better does not take place until the leaders of the warring camps leave the battlefield for the conference room. Grievances are then finally directly addressed, at least tentatively resolved, and peace and order are restored. Common sense, reason and humanity finally prevail!

While this has been the traditional course of events, and still is so in today's world, it is high time that the destructive and useless war prelude become a thing of the past. Diplomacy, boycott, sanctions, arms embargo and the conference table and not war, should be the prevailing response to serious national and international discord. The world would be the better for it!

When Egypt's freedom-minded masses angrily demanded the resignation of President Mubarak and the dissolution of his repressive regime, America wisely chose to remain on the sideline, opting for encouragement, promise and threat rather than for military intervention. Thanks to this minimal foreign interference in its affairs, Egypt was able to embark on a road of change that promises to lead to greater freedom and to a democracy of its own making. President Mubarak was compelled to resign, his regime collapsed and a transition government is preparing the way for a freely-elected parliament and a liberalized constitution.

Tunisia had set an example for Egypt and the world. Torn by rebellion and left to its own devices, it had a short time earlier managed to avoid civil war and was successfully resolving its own socio-political problems in its own way. Tunisia and Egypt are clearly examples that other countries in upheaval and intent upon greater freedom and more democracy should emulate.

Libya is quite another story! When disenchanted, angry and change-minded Libyans took up arms in large numbers against their autocratic President Khadafy, America opted for military intervention, allegedly to prevent a mass slaughter of Libyan civilians, to effect a change of regime, and to fight the good fight for freedom and democracy. Under the auspices of the United Nations and NATO and with the support the England and France, America began its missile and air strikes to destroy Khadafy's military bases, airfield and supply lines, and should these air attacks fail to persuade Khadafy to mend his ways—and that is more likely than not—the no-fly zone approved by the United Nations will undoubtedly be extended to a no-drive zone that is likely to end in a ground invasion and a prolonged war. Shades of Afghanistan and Iraq! A repetition in variation!

Hindsight should have warned America against military intervention of any sort, and common sense and reason should have persuaded the United Nations to follow the more peaceful road of diplomacy, boycott, sanctions and arms embargo to bring freedom and democracy to Libya. When will the world learn that violence only begets more violence!

First Tunisia, then Egypt and now Libya! Can the likes of Bahrain, Yemen, Syria, Morocco, Ivory Coast, Jordan and Saudi Arabia be far behind in the current global march of freedom and democracy? Not likely! Things have already begun to rumble in the absolute monarchy of Bahrain, and autocratically ruled Saudi Arabia has already dispatched troops to help quell the budding rebellion. Despotic President Saleh of Yemen is scrambling to hold his rebellious subjects in check. Morocco continues to be a tinderbox despite recent political reforms, the Ivory Coast is a powderkeg about to explode, the streets of Jordan's capital have begun to seethe with discontent, and President Assad of Syria has chosen to have pro-democracy demonstrations dispersed with live ammunition.

Military intervention in the populist uprisings in these countries alone—even sequential commitment—is quite beyond America's prowess, and moreover sheer folly. Selective invasion is likely to target enemy (e.g. Syria) rather than friendly autocracies (e.g. Bahrain, Yemen). Such adulteration of the democracy-freedom cause reeks of flagrant hypocrisy and would deservedly attract international reprobation.

Like America, the United Nations and NATO are incapable of intervening militarily whenever and wherever there is social upheaval, and should also not intervene selectively and for the same reason that America should abstain from doing so.

On the other hand, peaceful sideline intervention by whatever country or league of nations—to protect civilians and to further the cause of freedom and democracy—is always possible and is morally advisable in any populist insurrection. Diplomacy, boycott, sanctions, arms embargo and peace-keeping troops may prevent the outbreak of violent civil unrest, or failing to do so, contain hostilities and minimize slaughter and destruction.

Wars of whatever kind are a primal and primitive response to alleged threat or need or greed. All wars are wrapped in self-righteousness, are all too often tainted by questionable ulterior motives and no camp ever emerges from any war the better for it. If mankind does not curb its propensity for violence, it will very likely eventually destroy itself.

Loose the hounds of war and all hell breaks loose.

The clock is ticking!

America: A Tragicomedy

America of today is something of a large-scale stage on which a national drama is being enacted. Informed and thoughtful observers of this on-going drama are likely to be both quite amused and very distressed.

They are amused by the unabashed commitment of the many to little other than a plethora of exciting competitive sports, to television's light entertainment, its breezy talk and engaging reality shows and its thrilling murder mysteries, to the characteristically frivolous novelties of the Internet, to the electronic world's steady flow of enticing gadgets, and to the joys of consumerism. Discerning observers can only conclude that for the many all-absorbing pleasurable distraction is clearly the order of the day.

Thoughtful observers are, in turn, deeply distressed by the lack of active interest on the part of the many in society's more serious matters: its prevailing political apathy, its little interest in the complexity of economics and in the commonweal, its disinterest in the improvement of national health care, its indifference to overdue prison reform and its wanting preoccupation with education. It is quite obvious to all observers that the involvement of the many in these and related matters of vital social concern rarely extends beyond passing grumbling.

America's many are clearly given to fleeting frivolous pleasures and too little taken with serious social obligations. Broad exclusive pursuit of all things titillating is the stuff of comedy and utter neglect of most things serious makes for tragedy. The result is *tragicomedy*.

America is an example of tragicomedy on a grand national scale, a social phenomenon that spells cultural decline.

The Romans wined and dined, frolicked and rejoiced while their empire was crumbling around them.

Mankind's Sisyphian Existential Lot

*L*ife's existential trials, tribulations and imponderable mysteries have plagued mankind since time immemorial. For centuries, our Western World sought and found comfort in philosophy and religion. Such is no longer the case. Thanks to the wear and tear of time, both of these sources of succor have by and large dried up. Both have virtually become antiquities, and need and longing for comfort and solace have been replaced by a passion for analgesic distractions.

The attractions of the material world have become America's addictive distractions. Foremost among these popular fascinations are consumerism, entertainment, sport and the Electronics Age's plethora of gadgets. These time-and energy-absorbing distractions have left little room for ought else. Today's Americans are literally revelling obliviously in their bubble of intoxicating distractions. This bubble of distractions, born of irrational exuberance, will after some time surely burst, as did America's recent financial bubble and as bubbles always do. Chaos will follow and then the cycle will begin anew.

In this *tête-à-tête* with the trying human condition and with their eventual fill of opportunistic distraction, Americans—as mankind characteristically does—will gradually revert form their futile binge in the physical world to a new metaphysical quest for solace and comfort. What new religious and philosophical thought this ultimate return to metaphysics will spawn is beyond our ken. And with this return to the transcendental, the grappling with life's troubling exigencies will have come full circle.

In the course of history, this pendulation in mankind's persistent efforts to make the human condition more tolerable has left a trail of emerging and dying cultures behind it. Each culture is spawned by metaphysical preoccupation and peters out in frivolous physical distraction. Cultures and civilizations owe their being and their demise to mankind's innate drive to make life more tolerable.

Like Sisyphus in Hades, mankind on earth is doomed to keep rolling its stone uphill only to have it keep rumbling back down.

Wars and Intervention

Wars of whatever kind have become passé. They are utterly futile, leave nothing but slaughter and destruction in their wake, solve nothing and only sow seeds of animosity that sprout yet more violence.

It is high time that wars give way to the peaceful sideline intervention of such international institutions as the United Nations. With recourse to diplomacy, boycott, sanctions, arms embargo and peace-keeping troops, opponents at loggerheads could be brought to a negotiating table presided over by representatives of the UN. There representatives would have to maintain a strict neutrality. Theirs it would be to facilitate and to moderate and not to judge. To dwell on guilt or innocence would only exacerbate matters and prolong argument. Solely issues relating to a war in progress or to imminent hostilities should be on the table for discussion.

Nations in conflict and factions in civil unrest must be compelled to settle their differences peacefully but must also be permitted to do so in their own way and to their own satisfaction. Under no circumstances should the intervening international advocate of peace take sides or dictate the terms of any final peace settlement.

To succeed in its mission, peaceful intervention must be impartial, compelling and persistent. It is more than high time that mankind have recourse to this civilized approach to human contentiousness.

Peace by peaceful intervention!

Empires Come and Empires Go

*E*mpires have come and empires have gone in both rapid and slow succession since time immemorial. They mark the troubled course of human history, a history scarred by wars, conquest and exploitation. Empires have characteristically emerged in a blaze of military victory, have prevailed haughtily until they lost their vitality, decayed internally and were replaced by or succumbed to yet another upstart empire-bound nation. History then repeated itself and keeps on repeating itself.

Brief reference to but a selection of history's touted empires is enough to evidence the timeless and universal lure of power, domination and wealth and the ultimate failure of national subjugation and exploitation.

Egypt's ancient kingdoms (3100–1567 B.C.) gave way to the powerful Egyptian New Empire that managed to last until the 7th century B.C. The Assyrian Empire dominated the Middle East in the 8th and 7th centuries B.C., the Persian Empire moved into the forestage in the 6th century B.C., and the Empire of Alexander the Great outshone all other nations in the 4th century B.C. The Turkish Ottoman Empire (14th to the 20th century A.D.) was the last and geographically the most expansive of these mideastern empires. Each of these empires had its eyes focussed vainly on eternity!

The Roman Empire, the first and arguably the most prominent of the many empires associated with Europe, prevailed from the first century B.C. to the 4th century A.D. A rush of colonial empires— among them, the Spanish, Portuguese, Dutch, British and French— followed the discovery of the Americas (1492–). The Czarist (1721–), the Austro-Hungarian (1867–) and the German (1871–) empires were victims of the First World War (1914–18), and the brief upstart empires of Adolf Hitler (193–) and Benito Mussolini (1935–) crumbled in the Second World War (1939–45).

Except perhaps for their less ferocious pursuit of imperial power and their less tyrannical governance, and except for the greater civility of the British Empire (1604 to the middle of the 20th century), these

Europa-based empires differed little from their earlier mideastern counterparts. Expansionsim, conquest, oppression and exploitation continued to characterize empire building. And like all their predecessors, these latter-day empires came and went, leaving more havoc than blessing in their wake, more pain than joy.

The history of the East, like the histories of the Middle East and of Europe, is the history of a succession of empires. The empires of China began with the short-lived Ch'in Empire (221–207 B.C.). The Han Empire (202 B.C.–221 A.D.) that followed rivalled the Roman Empire in size, power and wealth. For several centuries, overlapping minor empires followed in rapid succession. Then major empires dominated from the 7th century on: the Tang 9618–906), the Sung (960–1279), the Yuan (Mongol-Chinese, 1280–1368) and the Ming (1368–1644). the following Manchu Empire (Ch'ing Dynasty (1644–) gave way in 1912 to a restive Chinese Republic.

Both major and minor Chinese empires had for centuries been incessantly wracked by civil wars and devastated by wars of expansion and of defense. Unfortunately, this turmoil did not end with the demise of Imperial China. With the collapse of the Manchu Empire in 1912, China, plagued anew by feuding rival military factions, quickly disintegrated politically. Unity and order were not re-established until the formation of the Peoples Republic after the Communists, led by Mao Tse-tung, defeated the Nationalists, under Chiang Kai-shek, in the civil war of 1946–49.

It was not until on in the 7th century A.D. that Japan began its transition from a clan to an imperial structure of governance patterned largely after Chinese imperialism. Until the middle of the 12th century, short-term insignificant emperors and empresses came and went in rapid succession. They reigned passively, powerful and ambitious regents ruled absolutely. Civil war ended the regent period and paved the way for the shogunate centuries that followed. Dictatorial shoguns, militaristic feudal overlords, ruled the roost and its emperors until the emergence of the Meiji Empire (1868–1912). Absolute imperial power then fell into the hands of Emperor Yoshinobu.

By 1912, following successful wars with Korea (1894), China (1894) and Russia (1904), Japan was the strongest military and imperialist power in Asia. Continuing to flex its growing might, it occupied Manchuria in 1932, invaded China again in 1937, Indochina in 1940, and then attacked Pearl Harbor in 1941. Imperial Japan was now at the peak of its power. Defeat in the Second World War (1939–45) left the Japanese Empire decimated. Japan was occupied and democratized, and its emperor's imperial power was reduced to ceremony and symbol. Like China's history of imperialism, Japan's centuries of imperialist rule were marked by constant turmoil. Political quest for power and wealth led to incessant wars of aggression and defense, to the occupation and exploitation of neighboring countries, to internal rebellions and wars, and all ended in national disaster.

The many empires of India differed little from their perpetually warring Chinese and Japanese counterparts. From the 4th century B.C. to the 19th century A.D., apart from many minor counterparts, some six major empires held sway: the Mauryan (321–185 B.C.), the Sunga (185–72 B.C.), the Andras (2nd and 3rd centuries A.D.), the Gupta (4th to the 6th century A.D.), the Bengalese (8th to 12th century A.D.) and the Moslem Mogol Empire from 1526 to 1857. India then became part of the British Empire, and finally a democratic republic in 1950.

India's metamorphosis from empire to democracy, like Japan's, was a progression from continuous imperialist strife, subjugation and exploitation to relative peace and security.

Such has been the international imperial road of mankind's national pursuit of power and wealth, and such is likely to continue to be the case. America is only the latest of history's most dominant empires, and it too will eventually go the way of all things—sooner more likely than later.

America became unmistakably empire-bound after the Spanish-American War of 1898 and in the person of Theodore Roosevelt, president of the U.S.A. from 1901 to 1909. In but a few years, a host of military interventions (Philippine Insurrection, 1899–1902, Moro Wars, 1901–1913, Panamanian Civil Strife, 1909, 1912, 1918;

Russo-Japanese War, 1905; Nicaraguan Civil War, 1909–1912, 1912–1917; Banana Wars, 1909; Mexican Revolt, 1914–1915; Haitian Revolt, 1915) made a veritable *Mare Nostrum* of the Caribbean Sea, and America's presence began to be felt in Southeast Asia and in the Far East. And with its successful participation in the First World War (1917–1918), America emerged a Western power to be reckoned with. After several more subsequent minor military interventions (Haitian Wars, 1918, 1934; Nicaraguan Civil War, 1925–1933; Banana War, –1933) and with the crushing defeat of the Italian, German and Japanese empires in the Second World War (1941–1945), America became the world's militarily most powerful nation. And with its succession of aggressive major and minor wars from the middle to the end of the 20th century—despite their mixed outcomes—America emerged the world's latest most powerful empire.

America's rush for imperial-world supremacy began with its invasion of South Korea in 1950. The Korean War stalemated in 1953 and was followed by the disastrous Vietnam War that dragged on from 1961 to 1975. Turning its attention to the Middle East after a brief lull in warfare, America sided with Iran in the Iran-Iraq War (1980–1988). American bombers then pounded Libya in 1981 and again in 1988 for its alleged support of terrorists, and the American Marines who had taken part in the Lebanese Civil War in 1958, intervened again in 1982.

America was no less intent upon its political expansion in the Western Hemisphere. In 1961 (Bay of Pigs) it attempted to overthrow Cuba's Fidel Castro and in 1965 it intervened militarily in a civil war in the Dominican Republic. From the seventies to the nineties it participated in the Salvadoran War (1977–1992) and in the Honduran Guerrilla War (1981–1990) and intruded militarily in Nicaragua's chronic civil wars (1978–1979, 1982–1990). America also invaded Grenada in 1985, Panama in 1989 and Haiti in 1994.

Having entrenched itself firmly in Central America, the U.S.A. returned to unfinished military business in the Middle East. Iraq was laid waste but not conquered in the Persian Gulf War (1990–1991) and a formidable military intervention in a Somalian civil war (1992–1994) was abortive. While still floundering in Somalia, America extended its military-political interventions to Yugoslavia, where it managed to burnish its tarnished imperial hegemony both in the Bosnian Civil War (1992–1995) and in the Serbia-Kosovo Civil War (1998–1999).

After the bombing of the World Trade Center in New York in September of 2001, America invaded Afghanistan determined to dispose of Osama bin Laden, to destroy his Al Qaeda terrorist training camps, and to overthrow the Taliban regime—and allegedly to spread American democracy and freedom. It was, of course, a rare opportunity to spread America's empire-minded hegemony to the very borders of Russia, America's long-time adversary. Today, ten years later, that war is still raging!

Convinced that the war in Afghanistan would be of short duration and determined to extend American hegemony in the Middle East, President G. W. Bush ordered an invasion of Iraq in March of 2003. Victory was swift and by the end of 2003, the country was fully occupied. But today, eight years later, the country is still in civil turmoil and American troops are still involved in military action!

The turn of the century brought with it an unmistakable change in America's imperial fortunes. The American Empire began to show distinct signs of wear and tear. America's expensive army bases strategically located in some 150 countries and its militarily and financially costly alliances with such strategically located countries as Egypt, Pakistan, India, the Ukraine, Kazakhstan, Georgia, South Korea and Taiwan (to counter such potential foes as Russia, China and Iran), the never-ending costly wars in Afghanistan (2001–) and Iraq (2003–), persistently threatening Islamic terrorism (2001–), the financial breakdown of America's financial world (2008–), and its most recent military involvement in Libya (2011), have left the country militarily overextended, financially drained and emotionally in turmoil. Mighty America has begun to teeter on its pedestal. Deconstruction is in the offing.

Empires come and empires go and *Imperium Americanum* will be no exception!

The Financial and Labor Worlds

*A*merica's world of finance and its world of labor have always been at loggerheads. Each has always been intent upon checkmating the other for advantage. Theirs has been a conflict of goals: ever more profit for the financial world and ever more rights for the working world. Neither has ever been particularly scrupulous in its pursuit.

Before the 20th century, capital clearly had the upper hand in their relationship. With the advent and rapid spread of America's labor unions in the 20th century, the working world came to the fore and began to assert itself both in Washington and at the work place. Increased governmental regulation of the financial world's industries briefly promised a balance of power. Subsequent legislative deregulation at the end of the 20th century tipped the scales in favor of freebooting capitalism. Untethered capitalism's irrational exuberance contaminated all America and everyone wallowed in a mirage of prosperity until the financial bubble burst and there was no money to pay the piper.

America could have been spared this painful financial collapse had both the financial and labor worlds been less given to their conflicting sectarian interests and had they together been more mindful of the commonweal. Each preferred to stress its primacy and its indispensability, come hell or high water. For each camp to continue to do so is only to perpetuate America's seven-to-ten-year unsettling pattern of economic ups and downs.

For either of these societal stalwarts to claim the primary role in their country's economy is but an academic exercise. Given our world's present-day economic structure, the financial and labor worlds are inseparably linked and interdependent, neither can exist without the other and production depends upon their interplay. The egg is just as important as the chicken and vice versa. Our economy depends on both money and brawn!

To be stable, an economy has to be a fair economy: the financial world has to moderate its passion for profit, the world of labor has to

Essayistic Ventures and Topical Asides

be content with a less than ideal workplace, their traditional mutual opposition must give way to mutual cooperation and both camps must become seriously mindful of the commonweal. But for such changes, America's economic welfare will continue its old and wild roller-coaster course.

To expect any positive change without the prod of appropriate new legislative regulations, is to expect the impossible. It remains to be seen whether Washington will rise to the occasion!

The Arab Spring: A Plus and a Minus

The so-called Arab Spring is darkening Israel's future. The Israelis and the Palestinians have been unable too long to settle their differences. An awakened Arab world is likely to break the impasse in short order. Present widespread upheavals in the Middle East promise to end in a more cohesive Arab world, one supportive of the Palestinians and hostile to Israel. America will then find itself in a bind. For the USA to continue its unabashed support of Israel would mean to court the disapproval of an increasingly more powerful Arab World and to jeopardize its hegemony in the Middle East. Expediency would then dictate a shift in America's foreign policy. Israel would cease to be an American protectorate, would be left to fend for itself and would, as a nation, inevitably be reduced to the same wretched economic and socio-political mess to which it had reduced the Palestinian state.

To date, and thanks to America, the Israelis have been able to assert themselves and to dominate what was old Palestine. In the not too distant future, and thanks to the Arab World, the Palestinians will likely be able to assert themselves and in turn dominate what was old Palestine. The former has been disastrous and the latter is likely to be no less disastrous!

What has been good for the Israelis has been bad for the Palestinians, and what will be good for the Palestinians is likely to be bad for the Israelis. Every plus appears to have its minus!

Technology and Sobriety

*P*ast ages, given primarily to philosophy and religion, were worlds shaped and run by greybeards. Metaphysics and belief were territory to which youth could only aspire. How times have changed! The elderly and their old pursuits have become passé, have had their day and have faded away. An upstart generation of youngsters in their twenties gave free rein to its wits and imagination and proceeded to reshape our cultural and business worlds, leaving only the troubled political arena in the hands of the elderly. These brilliant and enterprising apostles of cultural transformation managed to alter 20th century society radically from top to bottom by ushering in an exuberant and compelling Electronics Age. In its both serious and playful inventiveness, this adventure in electronics has "Pied Pipered" both young and old. The brilliant novelties, seductive distractions and the amazing scientific and medical benefits of this digital culture have dampened all interest in things philosophical and religious. Ours has definitely become an age of ingenious youth and astounding technology.

The *condition humaine*, once the centerpiece of thoughtful concern, has yielded to more mundane interests and pursuits. Philosophy and religion have almost become antiquities. This is too high a price to pay for a technological Utopia. How long will it be before this widespread and all-absorbing infatuation with technology becomes a rational relationship?

The tail is wagging the dog!

American Realpolitik and Libya

*P*olitical America viewed the Arab Spring of 2011 with more alarm than joy. Popular uprisings in the Arab world would change the power map of the area and could certainly diminish American hegemony in the Middle East. Alliances with such autocracies as Egypt and Saudi Arabia were, to be sure, slightly discomforting and morally costly, but they did guarantee America's influence in the Arab world. On the other hand, the Arab Spring's popular revolutions could see the emergence of regimes more inclined to oppose than to oblige the U.S.A. America could stand aside and let the Arab Spring run its course and hope for the best, or it could join and possibly exploit the fray. In Libya's Arab Spring, it chose the latter. America's manner of intervention in Libya was guided by its successful use of NATO in the Cold War with the Soviet Union.

It was a Europe decimated by the Second World War and threatened by an expansionist Soviet Union that gave birth to NATO in 1949. In the Cold War that followed, America both dominated and exploited NATO to checkmate its Russian rival. Given the success of this astute political maneuver and already militarily overextended in Iraq and Afghanistan, America again chose to use NATO for its own purposes, and this time, in the Arab Spring.

NATO was pushed by America to intervene in Libya's civil war to protect the country's civilians. Its actual mission—America's ultimate goal—was to bomb Khadafy's regime out of existence. NATO, with the U.S.A. at the command post in the background, did just that with its unhampered saturation bombing. Khadafy was out and el Keib, an American-educated Libyan—the Libyan national Transitional Council's American sponsored prime minister—was in. Thanks to NATO's American motivated intervention in Libya's Arab Spring, a potential decline of America's influence in the Middle East was averted.

America had used NATO to checkmate Soviet Russia during the Cold War and it used NATO again to coopt the Arab Spring in Libya. When and for what purpose will American realpolitik next exploit NATO?

Politics and Fear

America has the most powerful army, the strongest airforce, the mightiest navy and the largest nuclear arsenal in the world. It also spends more money on weaponry per annum than all other countries combined, and is the world's major exporter of arms. To guarantee continued popular support for this military might, America's political leaders have continued to argue that the country's security is threatened by enemy forces (e.g. Iran, North Korea, China, Russia and sundry terrorist groups). To foster fear of phantom threat has been a very effective psychological recourse of America's military-minded advocates of imperialism for the continued support of the American people. This steady support emboldened Washington to pursue a restrictive domestic policy and an aggressive foreign policy, policies that would suggest a country under siege and not a dominant world power.

America should take to heart President Franklin Roosevelt's sage reference to fear: "We have nothing to fear but fear itself." Fear, and particularly, phantom fear, should never be allowed to be a policy determinant. Fear has led America down a thorny dead-end street. It may not yet be too late for a change in psychology and for a change of mind with a change of course in domestic and in foreign policy.

Conflicting Institutions

Religion and Politics

*T*he church-state relationship in the civilized world has always been fraught with friction. In times primitive, religion and government were essentially one. High priests often became kings, kings often became gods and religion ruled. With the advent of civilization, distinct and separate conflicting institutions gradually emerged: the church with its purview of spirituality and morality, and the state committed to governance and law. Each of these polar bodies had its own agenda and each was primarily intent on intruding upon the other for its own sectarian advantage. Over the centuries, each of these societal partners was bent on dominating the other, and the tide of fortunes changed frequently until the end of the Middle Ages. With the Renaissance, the Reformation and the emergence of our modern-day states, this corrosive duel between the ecclesiastical and temporal worlds gradually became history. It became obvious that a country could not be effectively run by two disparate competing institutions. Church and state, two drawn swords, were separated, each left to tend to its own fief and to mind its own business.

The Financial World and Politics

Hardly had religion been sidelined, before government in the Western World, and particularly in the U.S.A., began to be assailed by a powerful new institution: an enterprising world of commerce. With America's transition in the past two centuries from agriculture to industry, its democratic governance became progressively more compromised by a spreading unbridled capitalism. By the end of the last century, the financial world's tampering in politics had become blatant, an encroachment very reminiscent of religion's earlier less than benign impact upon government. This intrusive, self-serving manipulation of congress has turned America's once-envied democracy into a deplorable plutocracy. Just as the church in the past had to be separated from the state, the financial world has now to be ousted from government. America can again right itself with a touch of its old resolve. It is high time for remedial legislative action!

Coda

Neither the separation of religion and state nor the banning of money from politics can or even should be absolute. Religion and the financial world are fixed societal realities, and as such can, will and should play a role in the electorate's choice of politicians and the electorate's legislative expectations. But neither organized religion, the church, nor organized money, the financial world, should be allowed, deviously or brazenly, to manipulate congress for its own express purposes.

Too influential a church spells theocracy.

Too influential a financial world spells plutocracy.

In both cases, democracy is shown the door!

Tax the Rich?

"Tax the rich" has in the course of the past three years become popular sentiment, a veritable mantra. The ordinary many have by and large become convinced that the wealthy few were not only responsible for America's present prolonged recession, but are also actually worsening it by not paying their fair share of the country's income taxes. Whether this is true or not will not be the focus of this psychological venture into economics. I have chosen instead to dwell on the possible impact a sizeable increase in the income tax of the very wealthy may have upon America as a whole.

Higher taxes on highest incomes would immediately reduce the income of the wealthy and add to the coffers of the government. More money could become available for education, medical care, public housing, social services and for the country's infrastructure. And if the wealthy were then to continue their present conservative investment policies despite their reduced income, the number of people employed would remain as low as it is today. In short, the lot of the many could improve somewhat, but the country's economic recovery would continue to be slower than desirable.

On the other hand, were America's financial world—in angry response to their reduction in income—to tighten its purse strings and adopt more hard-nosed investment policies, both it and the country-at-large would suffer a nasty setback. Reduced investment would further reduce the income of the rich, it would also add to the ranks of the unemployed, and the resultant decrease in income-tax revenue would more than nullify the benefit of the higher tax on the income of the wealthy, leaving the government even less money to meet the needs of the country.

A third major possibility—perhaps the best of all possible scenarios—would have the financial world dig in its heels, work ever more tenaciously and invest ever more widely and generously in a resolute effort to compensate for the decline in their income due to the higher income tax. This "I'll show you" response would benefit the wealthy few financially, would increase the ranks of the employed, and resultantly swell the government's revenue from income tax. The well-being of America as a whole would be well-served and its financial recuperation would be steady and fast.

Which of these three financial paths America's financial world may take if and when confronted by a higher income tax, is anybody's guess. The financial world's "do nothing different" response of the first of the above three possibilities would in all likelihood lead to a lingering, nationwide economic malaise. The financial world's truculently aggressive response of the second possibility would be financially disastrous for all of America. It is only the financial world's third possible response to a tax increase that holds America's sound economic recovery in store and promises a prosperous future.

For which of these three possibilities America's financial world will opt, when the time comes to react, will likely hang in the balance for some time.

A passive response is very inviting.

A reflex belligerent response is quite possible.

A tenacious resourceful response is unquestionably necessary.

For this third possibility to become the choice of the day will require psychological insight, prudence and good fortune. Taxes must and should be raised and the change in taxation should be large enough to begin to meet the country's financial needs and, at the same time, small enough to invite the cooperation and not vindictive opposition of the financial world. A challenge for both Washington and the world of finance! Success will depend upon a lot of good will and upon circumspect diplomacy and not political business as usual.

Time will tell!

A Painful Incongruity

America's much-touted open-mindedness and hospitality are not what they are purported to be. Fancy has definitely trumped fact. In reality, the attitude of the majority of Americans to the non-American—to the foreigner, the unknown other—has long been scarred by a highly disturbing incongruity.

Americans are inveterate tourists. Their long-time fascination with foreign lands, their peoples and cultures would reflect laudable curiosity and receptivity, and even admiration. This cannot, unfortunately, be said of the typical American's attitude to, and interaction with both those foreigners who chance to slip illegally into America and those who manage to immigrate legally. Once in America, the foreigner is no longer a person of curiosity and interest but one of animosity and disdain. The newcomer quickly becomes an undesirable job competitor, an undeserving welfare recipient, an added financial burden for our prisons, hospitals and schools. The foreigner in general, and the Mexican in California in particular, quickly becomes a favorite fall guy, the scapegoat who should and who is tossed out of the country on the slightest pretext.

Morally and economically, this maligning and persecution of the foreigner is clearly wrong and patently foolish, for the foreigner is certainly not a lesser human being and without him, America's farming, construction, restaurant and refuse industries would be in dire straits. Nevertheless, the foreigner has always been—and not in America alone—a favorite target for malice, a commodity not in short supply in the human community.

Foreigners are commonly of interest and acceptable, but only at a distance and not in our midst. In our midst, the foreigner is a lesser creature and not a brother, and we are not the better for it!

Today's Reality, Tomorrow's Hope

That ever more autos accommodated by ever broader freeways means an ever-greater spread of sprawls and scattered industries, ever more time on the road and ever more polluted air, land and water, is common knowledge. Though this disaster in the making will leave no one unscathed, all but a few of America's millions have chosen to see little, hear little or know little. The general public is too burdened by daily actualities to become preoccupied with future possibilities; the oil, car, construction and business worlds have a vested financial interest in a continuation of things as they are; and the political world is more given to its own immediate well-being than taken with the country's general health or with any dire future possibility. Only America's small cadre of climate scientists and a diverse scattering of tenacious environmentalists have persisted in sounding alarm bells.

These alarm bells have been widely heard but have as yet gone unheeded. Once heeded—better sooner than later—America will hopefully experience the awakening of a new social consciousness, and will see the emergence of a corporate and of a political world at least as mindful of the common good as of particular benefit.

Time has not yet run out!

Too Much and Too Little

Socialization once held sway in the Western World. It culminated in a dictatorial communism, then faded away. The Union of Soviet Socialist Republics exemplified this societal trend. The Soviet Union's demise saw the rise to international prominence of America's democracy, a government of, by and for the people, yet no less fallible and just as time-bound as any other socio-political structure. While Russia's communism had its more obvious Achilles' Heel, America has its less readily perceived mortal flaw. Too much government, too little freedom and almost total collectivization undid the Soviet Union; too little government, too much freedom and indiscriminate privatization are just as likely to undo America.

Freedom has long been America's most touted right, a veritable birthright. The individual American cherishes maximal freedom, America's control-shy worlds of commerce and industry insist on their freedom and vigorously oppose any and every government effort to regulate them, America's wealthy are free to determine the outcome of elections, and the corporate world's army of lobbyists in Washington is free to see to it that legislation is favorable to the interests of the business world.

In the past few years, this dogged insistence on maximal freedom to do what pleases or benefits has spread from the individual and from commerce and politics to virtually every nook and cranny of American society. An envisaged privatization of virtually every significant American enterprise would shrink government drastically and maximize freedom in one fell swoop. The disposal of America's garbage is already in private hands, postal service has already been partially privatized, as have highways, waterways, bridges and even the armed forces, and the privatization of public education, Medicare, Social Security and national and state parks has its ardent advocates.

Should this celebration of freedom and creep of privatization continue—as it is likely to—America promises to become something of a nation-wide bazaar of minimally regulated money-making enterprises big and small, and the Stars and Stripes and all it represents would appropriately be succeeded by a flying greenback. In this event, America's celebrated democracy will have gone the way of the Soviet Union's touted communism. Opposite socio-political ideologies would then have bitten the dust for the same reason. Had both camps practised moderation instead of opting for "too much or too little" each would have flourished longer and left a more admirable and laudable wake behind it.

There is still hope for America. It need only re-embrace moderation, that golden rule of which it was once more mindful. Had radical freedom, small and ineffectual government and sweeping privatization not become an intoxication, America's democracy would not have begun to be a full-fledged plutocracy. A return to the sanity of moderation can still right America's foundering ship of state.

Coda

Government enterprises should be primarily mindful of the common good, just as private enterprises are primarily mindful of particular interest.

Neither government-run nor private enterprises are by definition good or bad. Both can be either.

Enterprises of national, state or even regional significance are best run by government.

All other enterprises might best be left in private hands, and in either case, discreet moderation should be the guiding principle.

Needless to say, all functions best when there is least corruption.

Economic Growth

In America, economic growth has become synonymous with prosperity. Steady and ever faster growth has become an economic must. Stable prosperity has become a portent of stagnation and growth that slows or stops has become a harbinger of economic disaster. These are the self-serving pronunciamentos propagated by America's megalomaniacal corporate world.

Growth gives, but it also takes, and no less liberally. Economic growth does afford immediate prosperity, but pauseless rapid growth will inevitably peak in a bubble of prosperity doomed to burst in financial disarray.

An economy, the boundless prosperity of which depends upon perilous incessant growth, might best be replaced by an economy intent more on stability than expansion and content with the consequent more modest but far steadier prosperity. Life in America would become less tumultuous and Americans would be the healthier and the happier for it.

Spreading Autocracy

The long-time autocratic bent of America's foreign policy has become an ominous presence on the domestic front. Autocracy is nudging democracy aside in America and with surprisingly little opposition.

It happened analogously in the democratic Weimar Republic, and Hitler's National Socialism was the awful consequence. All that was done autocratically in Germany was done righteously for the fatherland, and the much that is being done undemocratically in America is justifyingly being done for national security.

Means are not justified by ends!

Invasion of Privacy

*P*rivacy in America has become a thing of the past. Secret surveillance—wire tapping, interception of e-mail *et al.*—legalized by President G.W. Bush's administration, is still the order of the day. That this clandestine monitoring of the nation for the sake of national security—a gross violation of America's treasured civil rights—has to date met with little more than spotty outrage, is incredible. Patriotic fear-mongering—terrorists are at our door—made acceptable what would otherwise have been absolutely unacceptable to the general public.

A change in sentiment is overdue. It is high time for congress to rescind the law that opened a Pandora's Box. Exaggeration and lies serve political purposes. The well-being of a country depends upon truth.

Prisons

*E*very country has its share of criminals. The number of its citizens a society chooses to incarcerate and the treatment of these wayward humans reflect that society's enlightenment and humanity to an alarming degree. Of all the western industrialized nations, America, a land of exceptional freedom, wealth and power, locks away by far, and for longer spells, the highest percentage of its people. This may suggest that America is a land of exemplary law and order, but may also, and more correctly reflect an unnecessarily draconian penal code. That

California alone, with its population of some 38 million, has more than 160 thousand of its inhabitants behind bars, while such a country as Germany, with its some 80 million people, has but 60 thousand locked away, gives cause for pause and responsible thought.

While America's overly abundant and over-crowded prisons are good cause for grave concern and serious thought, its ubiquitous solitary confinement facilities are depressingly disturbing. Solitary confinement of human beings for months, years, even decades is an all too common practice in America's many prisons. More than 80 thousand prisoners are wasting away in absolute solitude, and all too frequently, this inhuman torture ends in sheer madness. This socially condoned treatment of society's asocial members dehumanizes both the confined and the proponents of solitary confinement. It also solves no problems and benefits nobody.

Even when dealing with the worst of our fellow humans, thoughtful humane justice and not blind inhuman vengeance should be the order of the day, lest we lose our humanity.

Money and Politics

*I*n America's political world, the economy of influence is seriously out of balance. The corporate world's billions of campaign dollars, together with its plethora of monied lobbyists in Washington, guarantees a congress obligated to the financial world. The public domain, in sharp contrast, is splintered, has limited campaign funds and no spokespersons besieging the members of congress to support its many pressing needs and interests. Resultantly, Washington is literally and readily bought by the financial world. This compromising of the government has made a plutocracy of America's celebrated democracy.

The framers of the constitution envisaged a congress dependent upon the people and not upon campaign funds, a congress responsive to the people and not one beholden to special interest groups. These wise and esteemed founders of America would be appalled by their country's present-day political world.

"The best laid schemes o' mice and men
Gang aft a-gley."   (Robert Burns, *To A Mouse*, 1785)

Mankind and Actuality

Adam and Eve did not eat of the fruit of the tree of the knowledge of good and evil, but of the fruit of the tree of self-awareness and thought. And with this, their blind and blissful stage of evolution was done with. Their idyllic Garden of Eden went up in smoke and they were left shocked and deeply distressed by a new and very negatively perceived actuality: by their physical animality and by the harshness of life in a very imperfect material world. Mankind had now to adjust as ably and satisfactorily as possible to the adverse circumstances of this new stage in its evolution.

Beginning with Adam and Eve, self-consciousness and thought became and have remained for mankind both blessing and curse. Awareness of the self exposed our physical selves and thought quickly found our animality very wanting, indeed repugnant in many regards. Humans became concerned about their less than perfectly beautiful bodies, troubled by their nether regions and ashamed of their sexual appetite. The body had to be beautified, its problematic lower half had to be concealed, and coitus was dignified in marriage.

Appalled self-awareness and resourceful thought concluded that the fleshy self is less than beautiful, weak, sinful and mortal, and that life on Earth is but struggle, strife and suffering. Nothing was what it could or should be! Actuality had to be improved upon, and to make their wanting physical selves and their wretched earthly abode more sufferable, humans opted to diminish actuality and to embrace a preferred future virtuality, a spiritual possibility. In their embrace of a perfect spiritual self, they tried desperately and in vain to shed their wanting animality, and in their embrace of a perfect spiritual beyond, they vainly sought to blot out the trials and tribulations of their wanting physical world.

Heaven and its hosts have long been mankind's ideal possibilities and substitute for its questionably perceived wanting actuality. Unfortunately, this grappling with the human condition, though of some comfort and solace, has by and large been but an exercise in futility. An arbitrary negative view and too ready dismissal of actuality is evasion and not confrontation and valid resolution. It is high time that mankind, in its continued evolution, stop kicking the can down the road and choose to grapple with our human lot in a nondismissive and more fruitful manner.

Mankind could begin by viewing the physical self and our earthly life positively rather than negatively. Rather than dismiss our actuality in favor of a heavenly ideality, we might better affirm and embrace what is and make the best of it. This could result in something of a *heaven on earth*!

The Here and the Beyond

There is a Here. It is real, very messy and very wanting. There is a Beyond. It is, allegedly, very orderly and very perfect. We live in the Here, mankind's material realm. The Beyond, God's spiritual realm, awaits the righteous among us, or so we fantasize and hope.

These two worlds, essentially polar, are paradoxically of a kind. The spiritual Beyond, as envisioned popularly, is but a transfigured Here (the earthly immaterialized and idealized) and not a transcendent Beyond.

The Beyond, the Kingdom of God, is a monarchy, and God is its absolute sovereign. Ethereal shades of early-day earthly kingdoms and their rulers! God and his assistant hierarchy of winged humans (seraphim, cherubim, archangels, angels, etc.) rule Heaven as paternalistically as on Earth mighty monarchs and their lower-level layered aristocracies (princes, lords, dukes, barons, etc.) tended to their realms. The Beyond, like the Here, is peopled by both good and bad, and while the earth's perpetrators of crime are banned and left to rot in their dungeon prisons, the evil in the hereafter are relegated to the burning confines of an eternal hell. The questionable and futile wars of the Here will also have their more meaningful and more successful heavenly counterpart when the forces of God will do final battle with the demon-led forces of evil at Armageddon.

As traditionally envisaged, the Here and the Beyond, Earth and Heaven, are obviously not the polar pair they essentially are. The Beyond is by and large but a more burnished Here—just a "happier hunting ground."

So much for mankind's imagination or lack of imagination capable of transcending the Here. If indeed there is a Beyond, it deserves better!

Addendum

The Beyond of such as Islam, Buddhism, Hinduism and Confucianism is just as earth-bound as that of the Judeo-Christian world. And ancient Greece and Rome were both too taken up with and given to the Here to give the Beyond more than cursory attention.

More Common than Not

*I*ntimate relationships tend to go a characteristic course. At the outset, each partner is blinded by what are or seem to be the admirable qualities of the other, and each partner is blind to those attributes of the other that would cause alarm. In the course of time, shorter or longer, each partner's vision tends gradually or abruptly to flip. By the end of an intimate relationship, both partners have become blind to what once seemed the admirable qualities of the other, and each partner is blinded by what seem or are the attributes of the other that cause alarm.

Too many intimate relationships begin with joyous infatuation, only to end in troubling disenchantment. A little less *blindness* would make for a lot less tumult in these most intense of human interactions.

Religion and Philosophy

*U*ntil science came into its own in our modern era, religion and philosophy were mankind's major cerebral preoccupations. Religion left a wealth of mysticism and a wide trail of wars in its wake. Philosophy, in marked contrast, left a relatively frail tradition of thought and a world of books in its wake.

Mankind has always been more than ready to die for and to kill for belief. In contrast, mankind's commitment to philosophy and its truths has always been qualified and tepid. How is one to account for this disparateness? The answer is emotions! Religion taps emotions and philosophy depends upon reason. The emotions prevail and reason, when most needed, withers on the vine. Such it has been and such it is likely to continue to be.

Since man is first and foremost a creature of emotions, and reason is hardly more than a secondary pastime, the future promises to be but a variation of a war-torn past. Enlightenment will continue to linger in the wings of civilization's stage!

Our Freedoms

*T*o be free is the will of all living things. All creatures aspire to be free. Freedom is an essential ingredient of life. Such as these are common persuasions. There are, of course, innumerable kinds of freedom, and these freedoms, dependent upon circumstances, range in their degree from the rare absolute to the all too common highly restricted.

For mankind, all freedoms have been hard to come by and very easily lost. Freedoms of every ilk have been won and lost in countless wars and civil uprisings. America won its most cherished freedoms when it threw off the irksome colonial yoke of England in its War of Independence (1775–83) and when it promulgated its constitution (1788) and appended a Bill of Rights (1791).

Five freedoms were the foremost of these rights: the free exercise of religion, the freedom of speech, of the press, of peaceful assembly and the freedom to petition the Government for a redress of grievances. *Only* the fourth of these freedoms was qualified and wisely so: *peaceful* assembly. The remaining four were deliberately, and again, wisely so, left absolute, left for their successors to qualify in the years to come in accordance with circumstances and common sense. America's founding fathers were sensibly not about to crystal-ball future national exigencies and needs and limit liberties accordingly. Their wise restraint became a rather daunting challenge for an America that was to change rapidly and drastically.

Following the revolution, freedom and America quickly became synonymous and Americans since have proved to be reluctant to tamper with their iconic freedoms. Over the years, these freedoms have been tweaked or defined more closely only occasionally and only under compelling circumstances. Little more of import has been done than to curb seditious conduct and language, to criminalize such as the freedom to shout fire in a theater, to illegalize the religion-condoned circumcision of females and to question that of males. But for such as these infringements, the First Amendment's freedoms have by and large been left intact. In fact, America's cherished freedoms have not only been left more or less intact but have become more entrenched than ever, and its most treasured freedom of speech has actually expanded its sweep in a manner that would surely have left America's founding fathers dumbfounded and gasping for fresh air.

By the beginning of the present century, America's freedom of speech had morphed into *freedom of expression*, a subtle politically-colored expansion of freedom. This freedom of expression has opened the floodgates to questionable domestic and foreign possibility. It has, among many other things, legalized the Corporate World's financing of election campaigns and its financial control of Congress, and the Islamic World can now be freely and openly defamed and maligned. It is the latter that has emerged as a serious threat to the wellbeing and the security of America.

Essayistic Ventures and Topical Asides

America casually dismissed the furor Salman Rushdie's defamation of Islam (*Satanic Verses*, 1988) roused in the Muslim World, did nothing more than smile when the cartoons ridiculing the prophet Muhammed began to circulate in Europe, and most recently did little more than chide the Muslim World for its widespread terrorist reactions to the defamation of Muhammad in a film trailer posted on YouTube (*Innocence of Muslims*, film by Nakoula Basseley Nakoula, a Coptic Christian American).

Such apparent tolerance would seem to do America honor, except that it borders on folly, open invitation that it is for more widespread recourse to provocative disparagement in the name of freedom of expression, and for progressively more violent responses than just local terrorist reactions.

Following the scattering of violent anti-American upheavals in the Muslim world triggered by Nakoula's *Innocence of Muslims*, both Secretary of State Hillary Clinton and President Obama addressed the nation and the world. The venture was appropriate, but its extolment and stern defence of the Constitution's guarantee of free speech, its insistence that even hateful speech is no justification for violent reaction, and its but passing rebuke of the film and its maker, did anything but appease an outraged Islam. These pronunciamentos only stoked the anti-American sentiment sweeping through the Muslim world.

Unabridged freedoms are laudable ideal but not ideal practice, and this is particularly true of free speech. Our imperfect world peopled by imperfect beings has to settle for something less than the ideal, and that is for judicious curtailment of its venerated freedoms. And, to be sure, all societies have always, via law, either accorded freedoms to, or infringed upon the freedoms of their people, but unfortunately all too often inappropriately and inconsistently, and not always for the common good. Ku Klux Klan parades in black communities and Nazi parades through Jewish quarters were for some time deemed legitimate expressions of free speech. The smoking of, and trafficking in marijuana is federally banned but locally permitted. The circumcision of boys was recently banned, then quickly condoned in deference to

Judaism. The compulsory inoculation of children is widely regarded as a violation of parental right of decision. Nudity, a right of expression for some and a lewd and repulsive display for others, but for its permission in such as street fairs, festivals, parades and select beaches, has been strictly banned in America. Gay-cure therapy—another frivolous recourse to the First Amendment—has recently been banned, much to the joy of homosexuals for whom it was a damaging intrusion into their lives, and much to the consternation of the anti-gay segment of society for which it was, by some stretch of the imagination, a violation of free speech. Even the right of street people to sit or sleep on sidewalks has been abrogated in many of America's cities.

Such as exhibitionist nudists, street people and their annoying habits, the smoking of marijuana, the vaccination of children, gay-cure therapy and even hateful Nazi and Ku Klux Klan parades are civic, civil and medical matters, and should be dealt with as such and not as serious freedom issues. Not to do so is to trivialize the First Amendment.

On the other hand, the attempted censorship of books in America has been a serious violation and not a trivialization of the First Amendment. Henry Miller's *Tropic of Cancer* was banned from 1934 to 1963, Allen Ginsberg's *Howl* was challenged but in court found to be acceptable reading in 1956, and since 1983 some 12,000 other books have similarly escaped censorship; and in 2011 alone, concerned groups for moral, religious and political reasons, tried unsuccessfully to remove some 326 books from America's libraries.

While it has been wise of America to have no truck with an official Index Librorum Prohibitorum, it would be just as wise of her not to be absolutist in the embrace of the freedom of speech and of the press. Deliberately inflammatory mass communication that is likely to have widespread serious repercussions, would argue for some discreet form of censorship. Blasphemy, in particular, is a tinder box. Rushdie's *Satanic Verses* and Nakoula's *Innocence of Muslims* could and should have been dealt with more successfully.

Clearly everybody should be free to think, believe, imagine and feel whatever and however he/she may choose, but not regardless.

When this private world becomes public via such as speech, print, cartoons and videos, and deliberately to malign and to inflame, and when it is likely to invite violent responses, common sense would argue for a discreet and wise abridgement of freedom. The details of this abridgement—always situation specific—I leave to America's more informed, more experienced and more diplomatic heads than mine. The diehards of America's venerated freedom of speech should find some solace in the fact that this curtailment proposal is actually less a violation of the freedom of speech than it is a sensible regulation of action/speech. Potentially disastrous chain reactions are thereby nipped in the bud.

Freedoms and their limits are timeless concerns and problems constantly in need of review and adjustment to suit the situation and the times. This is a trying task in homogeneous cultures, an excruciating challenge in multiracial, multiethnic and multireligious democratic countries such as the U.S.A., and will be an almost impossible necessity in a globalized world of tomorrow. Adherence to a status quo nationally results in disruptive domestic upheaval, and adherence to a status quo in a globalized world would end in international disarray, a nasty foretaste of which we have just experienced in the Middle East. A practical interplay between the ideal and common sense has become imperative!

Consumer Spending

Consumer spending drives the American economy! Too much spending leaves consumers in too much debt, while the financial world wallows in its excessive profits. Inflated spending and profiting will inevitably peak in a financial bubble that will eventually burst and leave the country in a dire financial recession.

Too little spending leaves consumers debt free, while the commercial world is left teetering on the edge of bankruptcy.

To avoid disastrous financial recessions and painful periods of stagnation, moderation is in order. Moderate consumer spending and a moderate profit-minded commercial world would make for a relatively stable society.

Unfortunately, moderation in America is a virtue honored more in the breach than in the observance!

America's Heart

The poetic inscription on the Statue of Liberty—"Give me your tired, your poor, your huddled masses yearning to breathe free . . . " suggests that America did become something of the exceptional nation that John Winthrop (governor of Massachusetts, 1629–1649) in 1630 hoped it would become: "We must always consider that we shall be as a city upon a hill, (and that) the eyes of all peoples are upon us." Indeed, America has from its very inception been a beacon light that has attracted countless freedom-loving people anxious to improve their sorry lot.

Until the close of the 20th century, America's immigrants were primarily proletarian. America's vast farmlands and spreading industries needed and welcomed the entering brawn. With America's transition from an Industrial World to our present Electronics Age, its needs changed accordingly: brawn was out and brains were in. The downtrodden masses are no longer welcome. Their legal entry is exceptional and the illegals are in constant fear of deportation. America is today primarily interested in the highly educated immigrants needed by its Electronics world.

America is no longer the laudable haven it once was for the world's unfortunate many. The Statue of Liberty is no longer a beacon of light inviting the world's tired, its poor, its huddled masses. America has lost its heart.

A shame!

America's Financial Divide

America's unfettered capitalism has obviously been excessively good for America's enterprising capitalists. The veritable chasm that separates America's wealthy few from its vastly less fortunate many clearly attests to this. Since all legal attempts to hobble America's free-wheeling financial world have been quite abortive, cleverly countered or deviously circumvented, bold new efforts to cope with the situation are very much in order. Competition may succeed where regulations have failed. The corporate world's economic monopoly and its dire social consequences might well be countered and diminished by a widespread cooperative: a world of diverse large and small government-assisted cooperatives. Such a system could rein in America's corporations and make for a fairer spread of America's wealth.

Nothing ventured, nothing gained!

Marriage and Guns

Marriage and guns have become America's latest source of loud controversy. These new center-stage issues are unsettling a nation already otherwise seriously fractured. Both camps in each instance are intransigent in their embarrassingly irrational pro and con arguments. As usual, too, all parties are given solely to self-interest, and the commonweal is given short shrift.

Camps at odds must recognize that absolute rights and wrongs are things of the past, that judicious compromise should be the order of the day, and that the common good of society should be the determinant in any settlement. These guidelines would suggest a ready and fair resolution of the issues of same gender coupling and the proliferation of guns that are roiling America.

Same-gender *civil unions* with all the rights and responsibilities associated with traditional marriage should be legalized. Die-hard traditionalists will likely continue to be righteously upset by such a lawful pairing, but a deliberate avoidance of the word *marriage* is also likely to mollify them.

Gun control should be no less equivocating. All military assault weapons and facsimiles must be banned by law. Thorough background checks of gun buyers must be made mandatory by law. All guns must be lawfully registered. And the private resale or gifting of guns must both lawfully controlled and recorded. Such draconian measures will undoubtedly infuriate the National Rifle Association and its more ardent gun enthusiasts, but most of America's recreational hunters are most likely to be relieved and to acquiesce silently.

While this legal recourse to cope with two of America's many socially upsetting issues is unlikely to change minds and to end dispute, it can help to prevent controversy from getting out of hand, and does remind Americans that the commonweal must take precedence over factional interests.

Will Washington take the bull by the horns and address the marriage and gun issues effectively, or will it bog down in puerile bickering and simply kick the can down the road by having recourse to its usual feckless bandaid legislation?

Time will tell!

Technology and Unemployment

America is in a quandary. Technology has been a decidedly mixed blessing. A revolutionized industry has been both boon and bust. It has increased production and profit appreciably, and has unfortunately, at the same time, drastically reduced the labor force. Measures to counter this social scourge are overdue.

To begin to stem the present steadily shrivelling of the labor force, industry need only reduce the present working week from forty to thirty hours with no decrease in pay. This sharing of the benefits of technology should then continue into the future.

This proposed measure's 25% decrease in profit would certainly hurt America's capitalists less than the 25% increase in employment would benefit the country as a whole. And although this measure would undoubtedly not close the glaring financial gap separating America's few from its many, it could make the ultimately intolerable financial inequity less grievous. Many more remedial measures will obviously have to follow before America becomes something of a financial democracy.

That day is likely to be long in its coming!

Serious Thought

Thoughtlessness, half-baked thinking and conventional thought are the indolent or disinterested mind's recourses. Too many Americans never rise above this level of cerebral activity, are left wallowing in a nebulous maze of falsehoods, half-truths and disinformation, becoming easy pawns for the sundry questionable causes and political purposes of the reflective and enterprising few.

But that as many Americans as possible begin individually to reflect seriously upon personal, social and political matters and act upon these reflections, they may soon kiss goodbye to their treasured democracy and say hello to plutocracy.

Autocracies of whatever ilk are spawned when the many choose in indolence or disinterest not to become reflectively involved in personal matters and in social and political affairs. The thinking and active few take up the slack and shape the world as they would have it.

We will reap as we have sown!

Syria: Another Iraq?

War begets war,
Violence begets violence.

It all began *again* with a "rumor" of "alleged" chemical weapons, and predictably in but a few days, *again* with no corroborating evidence, diplomatic vagueness *again* morphed into righteous certainty. Shades of Iraq! President Bashar Assad's military had *definitely* had recourse to chemical weapons, killing more than a thousand Syrian civilians, including many women and children. Yes, Assad's regime had clearly violated an international norm, had ignored the Geneva Convention's banning of the military use of chemical weapons, and had obviously crossed the warning red line that President Obama had drawn in the sand some six months earlier. A country had committed a heinous criminal act that demanded just retribution. That American military intervention to punish a miscreant Syrian regime was a moral obligation, quickly became Washington's *sine qua non*. But a planned immediate air strike was put on hold when international support began to waver and when England, among other nations, chose to stand aside until a chemical weapons inspection team of the United Nations submitted its Syrian report.

Such was the moral outrage and prevailing sentiment in America the first week following President Assad's purported recourse to chemical weapons in late August 2013. Second thought then quickly persuaded a large and rapidly growing number of Americans that a retaliatory missile strike would likely lead to boots on the ground and then to yet another protracted war, and Congress, in turn, similarly persuaded, soon made it clear that it was unlikely, if requested by President Obama, to authorize any punitive retaliation. Thus, for America as of now, three weeks after Assad's chemical attack, retaliatory military action has become very unlikely. In the meantime, President Assad and the insurgents are continuing their gruesome war with relative impunity.

Common sense would argue that intervention of whatever kind might best be postponed until use or non-use of chemical weapons is beyond dispute. Corroboration of President Assad's alleged recourse to chemical weapons would, and certainly should shock the international community of nations to intervene, if only for humanitarian

Essayistic Ventures and Topical Asides

reasons. But what manner of intervention is likely to bank rather than to stoke the fires of this prolonged deadly civil war?

A punitive air strike by a morally outraged America, with or without the participation or approval of allied nations, would immediately but result in yet more civilian deaths, would likely leave Assad even more obstreperous and intransigent, and would do nothing to curb Syria's civil war. On the other hand, for the world's leading nation to allow Assad's moral and legal transgression to go unpunished, could be equally counterproductive: Assad would only gloat and continue his wanton ways, the civil war would rage on, and America's hands-off reaction would suggest impotence and lack of resolve, emboldening such renegade nations as Iran and North Korea to pursue their questionable domestic and foreign policies with little fear of any American reprisals.

America appears to be in a bind: damned if it acts and damned if it doesn't. Under these circumstances, it might best shift its attention from President Assad's assumed or actual military use of chemical weapons to a more important challenge: a termination of Syria's devastating civil war of almost three years.

What began as a religious rivalry, a relatively innocuous Sunni uprising to replace an autocratic Alawite regime (a radical branch of Shiism), soon morphed into a widespread civil war that pitted Sunnis together with a loosely affiliated motley array of fellow discontents (among them: The Syrian National Coalition; The Free Syrian Army, Syrian army deserters; and two Al Qaeda terrorist groups, the Jabbat al-Nusra Front and The Islamic State of Iraq and the Levant) against the Assad regime aided by Hezbollah, a Lebanon-based Shiite resistance organization supported clandestinely by a truculent and aggressive Shiite Iran. A very chaotic civil quickly became something of a more dangerous proxy regional war. Washington, as anxious sideline observer, had by then decided that an insurgent victory would serve America's interests better than a continued Israel-unfriendly Assad regime in cahoots with Russia.

What can be expected if both America and Russia choose to stand by and allow the Syrian war to run its course?

An Assad victory would leave his despotic Alawite regime even more firmly entrenched, would be a self-aggrandizing triumph for nefarious Iran, leaving Israel in mortal danger, would persuade Lebanon's fractious Hezbollah to become more aggressive than ever, and would leave Russia firmly based in the Middle East.

An insurgent victory on the other hand, would likely leave Syria's future in the hands of autocrats even more contrary and vicious than Assad and his cohorts, in the control of a mess of disparate factions vying with each other and dominated by two very militant al Qaeda organizations, would leave a backward plutocratic Saudi Arabia the Mideast's prevailing political power, and would enable America to tighten its political control and continue its economic exploitation of the Middle East.

Clearly, neither victory would mean a more peaceful Syria or a more stable Middle East. A war allowed freely to run its course holds little attraction. On the other hand, a military intervention by either the United States or Russia would make matters even worse. A *proxy regional war* could explode into an *actual regional war*, pitting Sunnis aided by America against Shiites supported by Russia. This eventuality would surely resolve none of the many differences, problems and disputes that have long wracked Syria, and would probably leave Syria and most of the Middle East a political economic wasteland.

An American retaliatory air strike would most certainly be counterproductive, and a civil, proxy regional or actual regional war can only be disastrous. Such recourses to violence to avenge or to change for the better have characteristically been exercises in futility. It is more than high time that military yield to diplomacy, and America, together with Russia, has an opportunity to break ground. And for this to begin, both countries must put their differences aside, must rein in their national and imperial interests, must stop their self-serving obstructionism in the Security Council, and must acknowledge the ultimate authority of the United Nations. A monolithic world organization could and should then begin a concerted campaign for peace in the Middle East.

A rejuvenated and more resolute U.N., with the full cooperation of both America and Russia, should quickly make a determined effort to persuade President Assad and Syria's splintered insurgents to lay down their arms, to admit an international peace-keeping force, and to remain seated at a peace table, together with representatives of the Security Council, the Arab League, and of Syria's neighboring countries, until most of their differences and problems have been satisfactorily addressed and fairly resolved.

To persuade warring factions to give peace a change is obviously no paltry challenge. But forthright, honest and fair negotiation with sincere assurances of adequate financial assistance to rebuild a country wasted physically, politically and economically, and with a guarantee that foreign interests would play no role in the decision-making, can be powerful inducements. Syria could become an example of successful international diplomacy. Nothing new ventured, nothing new gained!

It is clearly not for America to punish President Assad of Syria for his purported illegal and immoral use of chemical weapons on August 21, 2013. Such is *better* left to the International World Court at The Hague. It is also clearly not for any nation to intervene in such as the Syrian Civil War. Such is *better* left to the world's United Nations. Justice and peace would in both instances be *better* served.

Will a prudent America wisely stand aside in Syria, or will a heady America foolishly intervene, allegedly to duly punish President Assad's moral and legal misstep, but primarily to maintain its political dominance and economic advantage in an oil-rich Middle East? Is another Iraq in the making?

Time will soon tell!   (September 8, 2013)

Post Scriptum

Wiser heads and second thoughts have fortunately deferred an explosive situation. Thanks to an auspicious proposal by Russia, thanks to Syria's and America's acceptance of that proposal, and thanks to the willingness of both Russia and America to allow the United Nations to oversee Russia's proposal to rid Syria of its chemical weapons of warfare, America's threatened punitive air strike has been shelved and things in Syria have begun to change for the better.

As of the middle of September 2013, President Assad submitted a full list of Syria's chemical weapons and production facilities to the Organization for the Prohibition of Chemical Weapons, agreed to allow international experts access to all chemical weapons sites, and agreed to have all of Syria's chemical weapons secured or destroyed under the monitorship of the United Nations.

The United Nations inspectors are scheduled to be on the ground in Syria by November 2013, and all chemical weapons are to be destroyed or removed by the middle of 2014.

Thanks to international diplomacy, America's threatened punitive air strike has been shelved. Diplomacy's next challenge is the Syrian civil war. As argued above, the Assad regime and the insurgents must next be persuaded to lay down their arms and to permit an international body of troops to keep the peace. The two hostile camps must then be persuaded to sit down at a peace table to resolve their differences and to end the civil war.

If wise heads and common sense prevail, Syria could emerge the better for her devastating ordeal. If the civil war rages on, Syria will become a wasteland and the Middle East will be left in utter turmoil.

We shall see! (September 26, 2013)

Government and the People

Democracy is an idealistic form of government. While this manner of "people government" once functioned quite ably in the villages of New England (direct democracy), it stumbled awkwardly on the national plane (representational democracy). Nationally, government of, by and for the people quickly became compromised, and America's much touted democracy eventually became today's reprehensible plutocracy.

The structure of America's democracy has remained intact, but its functioning has been co-opted and corrupted by the corporate world. Elections, largely financed by corporations have left congressmen more beholden to their financiers than to the electorate. The wealthy have literally become the gatekeepers of Congress, determining as they do, who goes into and what comes out of Washington's august legislative chambers. The corporate world has benefited and the commonweal has suffered.

The collapse of American democracy was more inevitability than chance, given the quarrelsome, time-consuming and inefficient process that it became, and given human frailties and inadequacies. It is not at all surprising, that but for the political arena, the democratic process found little or no favor in any of society's other enclaves. Science, religion and the financial, industrial and professional worlds preferred, without exception, to function auto- rather than democratically. Ready expertise is obviously more widely attractive than the tardy vagaries of popular opinion.

Our founding fathers began America's experiment in democracy with high hopes. Unfortunately, ideal became a wanting reality that only became more flawed in the course of the following two centuries, and eventually morphed into today's abominable plutocracy. Like all other of the world's earlier attempts at democracy, America's fell short of its promise, and America's present plutocracy, if not appropriately modified, like all preceding pluto- and autocratic forms of government, is certain to leave social disaster in its wake.

America's democracy was only briefly, and then but half-heartedly, mindful of the well-being of all of its citizens, and its plutocratic transformation of today couldn't care less about the public at large. Both democracy and plutocracy have clearly failed to promote the commonweal. Failure in both instances is less attributable to a faulty political apparatus than to the wanting humans involved, both those governing and those governed. If both politicians and citizens had but been more informed, more reflective and more humane, either of the two political structures could have served the country as a whole both fairly and efficiently.

It is this general enlightenment of the American people as a whole that is necessary, if democracy is to be restored and to flourish in America. Merely to try to take money out of the political equation would be but bandaid and not solution. The solution is the enlightenment of America. America must become more broadly and better informed, more given to critical thinking and more humane than it is: a broad and long-term demanding challenge.

Will America rise to the occasion, or will it simply continue just to fumble blindly on? This remains to be seen!

Yes, fault lies more with the fiddler than with the fiddle.

Technology's Digital Age

*T*hanks to the Electronics Age, America was suddenly born anew. Callow youth supplanted age and experience, what was, quickly became passé, and a burst of fresh vitality began to course through the land, changing its cultural and financial landscapes, its work place and its play. Nothing has remained untouched by this tsunami of brilliant technology and enterprising youth. In one fell swoop, youth and digital technology moved from the shadowy wings of the theater that is America to a brilliantly-lit centerstage, and a brash entrepreneurism, characterized by restless imagination, focussed on startling innovation, and intent upon mammoth financial reward, became America's latest rage. The face of America that was, has changed radically and dramatically.

Dress in America's world of business, once quite properly conservative, has become deliberately casual, and professional interaction, once quite formal, has become comradely friendly. Corporate CEO's and their hired techies, dressed alike in their jeans, pullovers or tee shirts and run-of-the-mill shoes, have become indistinguishable and mingle freely. The corporate world seems to have changed for the better, appears to be less different and less removed from the ordinary many than in the past. Indeed, the dominant of the new-age corporations (among them: Microsoft, Apple, Yahoo, Google, Facebook, Twitter and Oracle) quickly became household names, and their CEO's (Bill Gates, Steve Jobs, Sergey Brin and Larry Page, Marissa Mayer, Mark Zuckerberg, Jack Dorsey and Larry Ellison) became billionaire celebrities almost overnight. This sudden name and fame and wealth was no happenstance. These Electronics-Age corporations and their leaders were immediately embraced because they exemplified what Americans have traditionally extolled (freedom of the individual, individual initiative and determination, and the possibility of the individual to rise from rags to riches) and because they offered America a steady stream of novelty, some of which is pure games and fun, and some of which is astounding innovation.

There is little in American life that the Electronics Age's internet has not touched or changed. Youth is taken with its myriad novel video games, and youth and age are given alike to the interconnectiveness of Facebook, to the telegraphic chatter of Twitter, and to the amazing usefulness of such digital devices as smartphones, pads, pods, tablets and phablets. The world of politics, of finance, of education, of commerce, of medicine, of science and of education are all no less taken with and given to this age of novel electronic means. Indeed, there are but few individuals in America who have remained relatively unaffected digitally, and no American institution that digital technology has not refashioned to good advantage.

Not surprising, the digital revolution has impacted America's language no less than it has changed the lives of individuals and the functioning of institutions. An exuberant youth opted for a whimsically imaginative mode of expression, and America's English has become laced with arcane neologisms. Facetious tech-company names (such as: Google, Yahoo, Oracle, Facebook and Twitter) herald the Digital Age's host of oddly-termed new inventions (such as: internet, web, network, iPhone, iPad, iPod, tablets and phablets), of fanciful associated verbs and nouns (such as: swipe, scroll, pinch, click, tweet, boot, skype , text, link, email and multitask; blog, browser, cloud, cookies, pixel, megabyte, cybertheft, herd, mouse and hyperlink), of quizzically-amusing expressions and mind-boggling acronyms (such as: storage in the cloud, to go online, to like someone, a microblogging tool, cloud computing, buy online and download to a cloud backup; BFN, BTW, BYOD, Wi-Fi, DDO, BFF, URL, CPU, WTF, and MPG).

To the digital-world illiterates, much of this boyishly-eccentric techie language is, unfortunately, virtually unintelligible. But fortunately, there is an on-line computer dictionary (webopedia.com) to assist the uninitiated. How much of this vibrant new-age jargon will eventually slip over into standard American English, remains to be seen.

The industrial revolution transformed an agrarian America and the digital electronics revolution transformed an industrialized America. Two drastic and drastically-different transformations!

The industrializing of America began early in the 19th century. It spread slowly from eastern and central to the western states until, by the beginning of the 20th century, the entire country was thoroughly industrialized. America then became and remained the world's leading heavy-industry nation until circa 1975. Begun by then, the digitalizing of America was swift and thorough. By the outset of the 21st century, the industrial era was history, the age of digital technology was in full bloom, and America was again the envy of the world.

The industrial revolution left no part of visible America untouched. Factory towns and cities became commonplace, railroads and highways began to link the farthest reaches of the country, farmlands shrank steadily, rivers were dammed, America became motorized, labor was mechanized, manufactured goods became the norm, and immigrant workers flooded the country. The visible material and human transformation of America was no less than astounding.

Though of a decidedly different nature, the Digital Age's transformation of America has been as thorough and as breath-taking as that of its parent revolution. While the industrial revolution focussed on mechanical innovation for its material improvement of man's life on earth, the technological revolution has been primarily intent upon improving man's mental well-being electronically. Industrialized America has literally been digitalized. The steam shovel and kindred tools wiped the seat off man's brow, the Electronics Age has relieved man's brain of arduous mental labor. The internet, websites, cloud, YouTube and sundry highly sophisticated digital devices have become indispensable in such fields as politics, finance, commerce, science, medicine and education. Such as Facebook, Twitter, Google, Zynga, Atari, Amazon and smartphones have facilitated communication, spawned social media, made shopping easy, and provided entertainment galore. An unbelievably utter and impressively positive transformation of America! To think that this digital technologizing of the country began but a couple of decades ago!

The industrial transformation of America was a blessing that did not come without a steep price. The country was environmentally severely marred. Factories left land and water contaminated and air polluted, and the heavy industries are at least in part responsible for our present inauspicious warming of the earth's climate.

The digital transformation of America has proved to be no less a mixed blessing than its industrial metamorphosis. The wonders of the industrial revolution blinded the world to its obvious ravaging of the environment. The wonders of the digital age have blinded the world to its latent negative human and cultural consequences.

That mass digital communication has already seriously encroached upon face-to-face verbal exchanges, should be a matter of grave concern. Both the well-being of the individual and that of society are at stake. Digital technology may indeed be able eventually to interconnect every person on earth, but it can only leave superficial contacts and not actual friendships in its wake. Meaningful relationships are dependent upon actual human and not virtual interaction. Further unchecked digital encroachment upon interpersonal communication can but end in a dangerous general social estrangement. The end result would be an ill-functioning society of strangers.

Too ready digital communication has furthermore had a negative impact on language itself. Instant telegraphic messaging and texting of one's every thought and action among both the young and old of America, has unfortunately left formal oral and written communication to wither on the vine. An abbreviated language, unmindful of standard English, seems to be rapidly becoming en vogue!

The Electronic Age's utilitarianism, that is, app-enablement, should be of no less concern than its digital communication. Its plethora of apps for countless purposes undoubtedly eliminates a vast variety of tedious tasks, enables very sophisticated new forms of investigation, and saves an enormous amount of time, but app-dependence, that is, wide and prolonged dependence upon these electronic aids cannot but diminish individual reflection and creativity. A moderate and more selective use of apps is overdue.

Youth is just as imperilled in its immoderate preoccupation with diversionary devices and apps as are adults in their excessive reliance on useful digital means. Too much time is wasted on such as chitter chattering on Twitter, frolicking on Facebook, indulging in Zynga's menu of entertainment, and enjoying the internet's myriad videos. When four to six hours per day are given to frivolous digital recreation, both physical and mental well-being tend to decline: sleep deprivation takes its toll and schooling begins to suffer. This bodes no good both for individual and society. Youth's rank indulgence in the fun and games of the Digital Age should clearly be curbed!

The education of elementary and secondary pupils *is being* negatively impacted by the digital world, and the education of university students soon *will be*. Online study has already begun to be introduced by a dozen or more American universities, and most institutions of higher learning are planning to follow suit. When actual universities are out of reach, online study is certainly an unadulterated blessing: it makes post high-school study for many who would otherwise have to forego further education. But when actual universities are within reach, substitute online study should be anathema. Distant learning, questionable convenience for students and financially inviting for money-strapped universities, can never be as effective as learning in the classroom or lecture hall. Should this axiomatic truth go unheeded, and should institutional financial need and digital aficionados prevail, the ultimate educational result would be unmitigated folly. Our present sociable and academically effective community of students, professors and administration could eventually become nothing but a campusless, professorless and studentless center for the electronic distribution of the canned learning of free-lance scholars. This very likely asocializing and watering-down of advanced education would clearly be detrimental to both the individual and society. Yet another good reason to be concerned about America's rapid digital transformation!

There are many other disturbing flies in the ointment! That the makers and shakers of America's digital transformation were by and large callow, uni-dimensional, single-minded, brashly confident, and blindly ambitious young men—albeit astoundingly imaginative, visionary, and creative—should quickly have become a matter of general apprehension. Older, better and more broadly educated, more experienced and wiser participants in the digital transformation, could have curbed its extremes.

The digital world's both play- and money-motivated ever more rapid rush of new and modified devices, gadgets and modes of transmission, has undoubtedly enthralled and benefited the general public, but it has also left it ever more ignorant of the inner working of digital technology. A spreading ignorance of the scientific underpinnings of this technology makes of the general public a blind and passive participant in America's technical transformation. This again can only be detrimental to the individual in particular and in turn, to the country at large.

The same can be said of technology's seduction of too many of the most gifted and highly motivated of America's youth. Too many other of society's vital enclaves have been left suffering from a dearth of talent. This imbalance can only have both immediate and long-term negative cultural consequences.

Thanks too, to digital technology's long reach, America is likely in the near future to suffer from a dearth of newspapers. The network's social media, an inexhaustible source of gossip, information and even more misinformation, is gradually becoming America's main source of news. Newspapers have already shrunk badly, professional reporters and columnists have already been discharged in large numbers, and the reporting of news has already yielded largely to advertising. The days of the traditional paper newspaper seem to be numbered, and neither to the benefit of the individual nor to that of society.

All of the foregoing and more does not bode well for America. The Digital Age's benefaction is enormous and the price is staggering. Digital technology's continuing uni-dimensional transformation of society can only in due time end in a cultural disaster. Technology of whatever ilk is but one component of a complex cultural whole. When part aspires to, and eventually becomes the whole, the result will be a uni-dimensional culture, a *technocracy*: a heaven on earth for techies, otherwise a bleak and barren cultural desert.

There still is time to avert this dire possibility! America's infatuation with digital technology need only be moderated.

The Mystery of Life

*L*ife, though commonplace, is without doubt the most abiding and most intriguing of mankind's many fascinations. The world teems with animal and plant life ranging from the largest of whales to the non-visible unicellular microorganisms, and from the gigantic redwoods to the tiniest of algae. Though ubiquitous in its manifestations, life itself has remained the world's mystery of mysteries.

We know of certain as little about the origin of life as we know about the origin of the cosmos. Genesis is imaginative narrative and the best of our philosophers and scientists have never managed to get beyond vague surmise and hypothesis.

When and how did inanimate matter become animated? That in a distant biblical beginning, God simply created the world and its creatures, fashioning mankind after his own image, and accomplishing all in but six days—once widely believed—has become but myth. That life just emerged spontaneously and mysteriously ages ago from dead matter, or that it simply came into existence supernaturally and simultaneously with matter and with the origin of the earth, is little more than fancy. That life originated billions of years ago in a fortuitous chemical reaction of matter, is more plausible but still only conjecture.

Neither wit nor imagination has shed much light on the *when* and *how* of life's origin and just as little on the *what* of life. Life manifests but does not reveal itself! Its myriad plant and animal manifestations are familiar to eye and mind, but *life of itself* is an invisible mystery. Theologians and philosophers have wisely tiptoed through the tulips, and scientists have discreetly chosen to leave well enough alone what cannot be dealt with empirically. To but deem life a miracle gift of God or a vital universal force inherent in animals and plants is simple declaration and not explanation.

Life's plethora of manifestations and their continuous evolution can be described and studied, its origins and its essence have been and will likely remain beyond mankind's ken. Such is the lot of reality's many imponderables.

The Brain and the Mind

*T*he brain, a long familiar organ, has of late been ably scrutinized by brilliant scientists of every ilk, its matter has been carefully analyzed, its structure duly detailed, and its consciousness, in all of its plethora of reaches, is being precisely brain-located. While the *what* of the brain (conscious animated matter) has largely been demystified, the *when* and *how* of its consciousness, like the *when* and *how* of life itself (see above, *The Mystery of Life*), have remained beyond the reaches of science.

Consciousness is to the brain what life is to the body, and both consciousness and life are beyond the *when, how,* and *what* of science. On the other hand, the manifestations of both consciousness (the world of thought and of feeling) and of life (animal and plant world) have been and continue to be a fruitful attraction for both speculation and hard science.

So much for the brain and now to account briefly for the mind. The concept mind has commonly been equated with the conscious or functioning brain. It might more precisely be termed the consciousness or the functioning *of* the brain. Theologians, philosophers and scientists alike have discreetly chosen to go no further than such designation in their limited preoccupation with mind, and for good reason. Consciousness, like life, is but another of reality's many imponderables, and imponderables, beyond mankind's ken that they are, have always been wisely or otherwise left to their own devices.

Art and Beauty

The Concept Art

*T*he word *art* bears more scrutiny than it has commonly enjoyed. Precisely, *art* is a concept designating a broad sweep of creative enterprises and not some specific thing created by some specific person, as generally conceived. This sweep of creative ventures comprises a variety of fields of accomplishment, among them, such as music, literature, painting and sculpture, and these, like the concept *art*, only designate areas of creative interest and do not allude to any specific works of art. In brief, *art* comprises many fields and only those engaged in these fields, that is artists, create *art*, or more precisely, works of art.

Like its Latin origin (*ars*), the English word *art* and its many compound extensions at times allude primarily to a *work* or *works of art*, at other times no less to creative skill, and then clearly to skill and product. Such as art collector, museum of art, art auction and art exhibition obviously focus on *works of art*. Such phrases as the art of evoking—of acting and—of writing are as clearly skill-minded as such words as artless, artifice, artisan and artistry. And such as work of art, field of art, primitive art and artist plainly allude both to skill and product.

Essayistic Ventures and Topical Asides

The Concept Beauty

The word that is most commonly associated with art is beauty. The word defines art! Yet, this word, the apparent essence of art, is less elucidation than it is challenge. What, precisely, is beauty? Such prominences as philosophers, writers and even scientists have since antiquity addressed the concept, but only in passing and rather evasively. Ancient Greece's Aristotle chose to focus on origin and not definition: "Beauty is the gift of God." (Diogenes Laertius, *Lives of Eminent Philosophers*, V). Centuries later, Ralph Waldo Emerson, America's essayist and poet, side-stepped definition just as deftly as had Aristotle: "One man's beauty, another's folly." (*Essays*, 1841). Unlike Aristotle and Emerson, England's John Keats commented on beauty, but settled for poetic exclamation rather than critical explanation: "Beauty is truth, truth is beauty—that is all/ Ye know on earth, and all ye need to know." (*Ode on a Grecian Urn*, 1819). In sober contrast, George Santayana, Spanish-American philosopher, candidly insisted that beauty was simply beyond human words: "Beauty as we feel it is something indescribable: what it is or what it means can never be said." (*The Sense of Beauty*, 1896). Thinkers of this persuasion, before and after Santayana, commonly avoided any reflection on beauty and resigned themselves to simple categorization. The poet-painter, Dante Gabriel Rossetti, settled for genius: "Beauty like hers is genius." (*Sonnets from the House of Life*, 1870–1881). David Herbert Lawrence, British author, playfully tossed beauty into the bin of mystery: "Beauty is a mystery. You can neither eat nor make flannel of it." (*Sex Versus Loveliness*, 1930). And Anne Sexton, American poet, opted for passion: "Beauty is a simple passion." (*Snow White and the Seven Dwarfs*, 1971).

This traditional dallying with beauty has proved to be a dead end. It is more than high time for students of beauty to begin to cultivate a more mindful view of their interest, one broached long ago but today still blithely ignored. For David Hume, Scottish philosopher and historian, beauty was in the mind and not of a thing: "Beauty in things exists in the mind which contemplates them." (*Essays*, 1741–42).

Hume's potentially ice-breaking drift of thought did not resonate. Nor did Margaret Hungerford's apt epigrammatic reiteration of Hume's persuasion attract any real scholarly attention: "Beauty is in the eye of the beholder." (*Molly Brown*, 1878). A necessary neuro-psychological assessment of beauty is not yet in the offing.

One might begin to pursue this promising new trend of thought by starting with art and ending with beauty: Art is an idea, an abstract universal; an object of art is particularized art, a thing of beauty; and beauty is an appreciative reactive feeling, a euphoric state of the mind occasioned by particular novel complex imprints upon the brain, such as a particular meld of colors and shapes (painting), particularly shaped solids (sculpture), choice language, imagery, rhythm and rhyme (poetry), a particular flow of sounds (music), and a particular sequence of movements (dance). Hypothesizing such as this will have to begin to attract the argument and reasoning of today's avant-garde biologists, neurologists and psychologists, if our prevailing scattering of simplistic views of beauty is ever to become a thing of the past.

Characterization of Art

Where human beings, there too, art, and this has been so since time immemorial! And where advanced civilization, there too, broad and ready interest in the nature of art. In the Western World, and particularly since the Renaissance, opinions have been many and varied.

Some of the Western World's many artists and intellectuals who have preoccupied themselves with art in general have attempted broad characterizations. For the English author Richard Franck, art and nature were interlinked: "Art imitates nature." (*Northern Memoirs*, 1658). For John Ruskin, English writer and critic, art demanded both body and soul: "All great art is the work of the whole living creature, body and soul, and chiefly the soul." (*The Stories of Venice*, 1851). Emil Zola, French novelist, maintained that art was a very personal view of reality and insisted that his own art was a candid censure of society and approval of the individual: "A work of art is a corner of creation seen through a temperament." "My art is a negation of society, an affirmation of the individual, outside all rules and demands of society." (*My Hates*, 1866). For Boris Pasternak, Russian novelist, art was risk and sacrifice: "Art is unthinkable without risk and spiritual sacrifice." (*On Modesty and Bravery*, 1936). For French author André Malraux, art was a revolt: "All art is revolt against man's fate." (*The Voice of Silence*, 1951).

Other students of art have been more specific in their pronunciamentos. The English dramatist and critic, John Dryden, paired nature and art: "By viewing Nature, Nature's handmaid art/ Makes mighty things from small beginnings grow." (*Annus Mirabilis*, 1667). Johann Wolfgang Goethe, on the other hand, made the personal the one and all of art: "Individuality of expression is the beginning and end of all art." (*Proverbs in Prose*). The French poet and critic, Remy de Gourmont, was convinced that love was art's blood and life: "Love is the accomplice of art. Take love away and there is no longer art." (*Décadence*, 1902). Joseph Conrad, Polish-English novelist, preferred to highlight the imagination: "Imagination not invention, is the supreme master of art as of life." (*A Personal Record*, 1912). In sharp contrast, Marcel Proust, French novelist and critic, boldly argued cause and effect between neurosis and art: "All the great things we know have come to us from neurotics. It is they, and only they who have founded religions and created works of art." (*Remembrance of Things Past*, 1913–27). Albert Einstein, the scientist, preferred to be more opaque than Proust: "The most beautiful thing we can experience is the mysterious. It is the source of all true art and science." (*What I Believe*, 1930).

Few of any serious students of art have over the centuries actually looked askance at it. Philippe Destouches, French dramatist, was given to observation and not denigration: "Criticism is easy, art is difficult." (*Les Glorieux*, 1732). Cardinal Newman, English theologican, was simply more impressed by nature than by art: "Living Nature, not dull Art/ Shall plan my ways and rule my heart." (*Nature and Art*, 1868). Ireland's flamboyant Oscar Wilde was but facetiously dismissive: "Art is quite useless" (*Dorian Gray*, 1891). And Georges Braque, French painter and close friend of Picasso, only found art less comforting than science: "Art upsets, science reassures." (*Pensées sur l'Art*).

Except for the tongue-in-cheek pronunciamentos of such as Destouches, Newman, Wilde and Braque, art has over the centuries been widely and unequivocally embraced, enthusiastically pursued and generously assessed, and this should surprise no one. Samuel Taylor Coleridge, English poet and critic, could hardly contain his lavish praise of art: "Now art used collectively for painting, sculpture, architecture and music, is the mediatrix between and reconciler of, nature and man. It is therefore the power of humanizing, of infusing the thoughts and passions of man into everything which is the object of his contemplation." (*On Poesy or Art*, 1818). On the other hand, Gustav Flaubert, French novelist, avoided all rhapsody by but tersely drawing attention to what he deemed the essence of art: "Art is nothing without form." (Letter of August 1846). For Ralph Waldo Emerson, American poet and essayist, the *raison d'être* of real art was unassailable: "Every genuine art has as much reason for being as the earth and sun." (*Society and Solitude*, 1870). For George Sand, art's purposes were primarily the true, the good and the beautiful: "Art for art's sake is an empty phrase. Art for the sake of the true, art for the sake of the good and the beautiful, that is the faith I am searching for." (Letter of 1872). Leo Tolstoy, Russian novelist, essentially echoed Sand's veritable religion of art: "Art is the human activity having for its purpose the transmission to others of the highest and best feelings to which men have risen." (*What is Art*, 1898).

Coda

The many and varied preceding *in nuce* definitions and characterizations of beauty and of art in general are anything but revelatory. Students of the fine arts, acknowledging that beauty is beyond definition, simply settled for categorization and paeans of praise that beg for explanation. Students of art, just as baffled in their grappling with art in general, settled by and large for broad characterizations, vague specifics, playful irony and hymns of praise. It is high time that artists, art scholars and sundry disciplines of art and beauty begin to ally themselves in interdisciplinary studies with the cognoscenti of disciplines relevant to art and beauty (e.g. aesthetics, psychology and biology). But for such a serious cooperative focus, art and beauty will, in their characterization, continue to be wrapped in irrational exuberance and fall short of credible explanation.

Autumn 2014

Addendum

Abstracts such as art and beauty have always been held at arm length rather than accorded detailed analysis. Actual works of art and beauty, on the other hand, have over the centuries and in sharp contrast, attracted persistent broad and thoughtful attention. There is, resultantly, no dearth of readily available insightful, information about the Western World's unique schools of art, bountiful works of art and plethora of artists, from antiquity to the present. While these schools, works of art and artists have and still attract the scholarly attention they merit, serious study of the abstracts art and beauty continue to be shunned. Hopefully, America's present-day ever more intensive interdisciplinary study of the brain/mind will provide the impetus necessary to end this neglect. The sooner, the better!

Duplicitous Word Games

Terrorism

When a given act against another is intent upon instilling horror and fear, and/or inflicting deadly injury, the act is one of terror, and the perpetrator is deemed a terrorist.

The definition of terrorism is not a matter of controversy, and terrorism and its practice are abhorred and universally condemned. Notwithstanding, terrorism has become a world-wide *cause célèbre*, a veritable battered football in a raucous international blame-game.

Terrorism knows no national, institutional, racial, ethnic, gender or age boundaries. It is perpetrated by anyone, against anyone or anything, and anywhere. The waters begin to muddy when wily words begin to fly reproachfully on all sides. The other, that is to say the enemy, is most immediately and commonly branded the evil perpetrator of terrorism, and innocence is self-righteously argued on all sides, or acts of terrorism blatantly become just retribution for injustices suffered. These self-serving accusations, professions and justifications have only added fuel to a fire already out of hand.

That the Western World has chosen to associate terrorists and terrorism primarily with Islam's perpetrators of violence and fear, and that the Islamic World has responded in kind, is simply a battle for words, self-serving politics, obfuscation and not clarification: obvious realpolitik. Each camp stigmatizes the other, the public at large is duped, and the perpetration of terrorism by both sides and in many guises, continues unabated. and nothing is likely to change until each culture becomes more informed about the other, becomes more reflective and humane, and until common sense and good will begin to prevail.

War and Lies

The global semantic abuse and nefarious misuse of the words terrorism, terrorist and terror, has been centerstage in America's very extensive and varied use of language to serve political and military purposes. Language became the first victim of war when it became an instrument of war. American military interventions in invasions of Panama (1989), Somalia (1992) and of Haiti (1994) became palatable "Operation Just Cause, Operation Restore Hope, Operation Uphold Democracy," and America's wars in Iraq (1990, 1998, 2003) became innocuous "Operation Desert Storm, Desert Fox, Operation Iraq's Freedom." These righteous-sounding euphemisms were clearly intent upon abetting America's questionable expansionist adventures.

A plethora of deceptive verbal sweeteners also managed to induce the credulous American public to passively accept its country's many international nefarious activities: The killing of civilians and the destruction of non-military properties simply became "collateral damage;" the removal of suspect terrorists to torture centers abroad became nothing more than "extraordinary renditions;" suspicious civilians became "enemy combatants" conveniently impounded uncharged in Guantanamo; torturous information extraction was but "enhanced interrogation;" and virtual drowning, the epitome of torture, became an innocuous-sounding "waterboarding."

Lies beget wars and wars beget lies! Saddam Hussein's weapons of mass destruction—a blatant Washington lie—triggered President G.W. Bush's Second Persian Gulf War (2003), and though Iraq was left devastated, not liberated and democratized, a pompous Bush took it upon himself, in May 2003, to appear on the deck of an American battleship in full battle dress to deceptively declare "mission accomplished." These bold lies served Washington's camouflaged agenda even better than anticipated: A war was deemed necessary to eviscerate an upstart dictatorship that allegedly threatened America's Middle East hegemony, and Washington's featuring of non-existent weapons of mass destruction, and Bush's "mission accomplished" were deemed necessary to placate the general public that was becoming progressively more disquieted by America's persistently militant foreign policy.

These perfidious lies were not simply chance figments of G.W. Bush's imagination. They were motivated and accommodated by Bush's "divine mandate" which, in turn, derived from "manifest destiny" coined in December of 1845 by John L. O'Sullivan, an editor of the *New York Morning New*. In his editorial, O'Sullivan argues that it was the Union's:

". . . manifest destiny to overspread and possess
the whole of the continent which providence has
given us for the development of the great
experiment of liberty and federated self-government."

Manifest destiny quickly became a widespread American conviction, a doctrine that fueled America's westward expansion and national consolidation, then lingered on, *sotto voce*, into the twentieth century until G.W. Bush began to exploit it. O'Sullivan's "manifest destiny" became Bush's "divine mandate," and to make O'Sullivan's doctrine relevant to America of today, Bush had only to shift its focus from a continent to the world at large and to substitute "Democracy" for "federated self-government." O'Sullivan's nation-minded exceptionalism had its rather innocuous fictive divine push, Bush's empire-minded exceptionalism became a divine shove, an outrageous lie. His argued "messianic mission" to spread America's touted liberty and Democracy throughout the world and however, was hubris and mendacity at their worst: raw imperialism was brashly satisfied.

Addendum

Language in use is never static. It never ceases to evolve both semantically and morphologically. Linguists have over the years ably described and amply accounted for their natural evolution. Language too, has always been deliberately contaminated, more or less, in various ways and to different degrees, and everywhere and at all times. This long-time and widespread appalling abuse and semantic distortion of language has in contrast, and by and large, been left begging for its share of serious attention. It is high time that this fallow field receive its merited scholarly perusal. My "Terrorism" and "War and Lies" do little more than broach the subject. The language of America's political world is replete with words that, like terrorism, have been and continue to be semantically distorted and questionably used, and laced with the myriad verbal sweeteners every war spawns. A thorough study of this political misuse and abuse of language is in order, and this study should be extended not only to the duplicitous use of language in the field of advertising but also to the all too common self-serving violation in such fields as finance, medicine, education and even religion. Such a study, or even better, such studies could reveal much about language and even more about humans!

What is Love?

The word love has had a long and rough semantic ride. Along the way, it became a coat of many colors, a coat obscured by its profuse and clashing colors. Expressed otherwise, this profoundest and most bandied about of human emotions, became over time a rock that never ceased to attract ever more obscuring moss.

At its purest in the early days of Christianity, the concept love apparently connoted nothing more than deep and selfless affection for another. The fellowship that bonded Christ and his disciples exemplified this purely brotherly love. It was not long before this core meaning of the word love began to become something of a coat of many colors.

In the English-speaking world, Christian love, a.k.a. *agape,* was soon obscured by a plethora of different loves ranging from the very ethereal to the very worldly. Courtly love, a knight's chivalrous devotion to a married lady of the court, was long esteemed, Platonic love, a sexless affectionate relationship, had its day, and romantic love, a lover's ardent courting of his fair lady, once a very fashionable affair, has almost spent itself. And such expressions as to make love (to engage in sex), love affair (sexual relationship) and love child (bastard), are at the worldly end of the love spectrum.

This polar semantic configuration of the word love has persisted to the present and has changed only in a shedding of its initial stark explicitness. In time and as the word love began to be used more prevalently and more freely, its two basic meanings became progressively more nuanced. Love, once a deep and selfless Christian affection, became, among many other things, a more worldly, warm regard for another, a mere fondness for someone or something, a simple pleasurable experience, and even homosexuality's once bestiality has become but another expression of human love. This semantic nuancing of the word love was complemented by the melding of love's polar warm affection and sexual desire in such expressions as to fall in love and to be in love.

This semantic proliferation of the word love is good cause for a reflective pause. But for some contextual elucidation, concepts such as love with its different meanings which, in turn, have their own shades of meaning, can only leave all too many listeners and readers somewhat perplexed or quite misinformed. Since precision and clarity are communication's first commandment, and since adequate contextual elucidation is rather spotty, it is imperative that English in general become a more finely-tuned instrument than it presently is. This is obviously more easily said than done!

Rather than simply adding ever more meanings and nuances to single words, English might better have had systematic recourse to appropriate precise neologisms. Such would clearly have obviated much language fuzziness. But then, language always evolves more capriciously than logically!

The Electronics Age

The Electronics Age has no cultural anchor: no history, religion, philosophy, psychology, literature, art, and no mythology. It is a thing-worshipping civilization that has turned its back upon humanism, is given to itself and taken with the present. Its means, that is to say, its digital paraphernalia, has become its ends. This is a world of youth's making, a technological age that is inundated by attractive and distractive electronic novelties, and that has unfortunately left both young and old enthralled.

This acultural aberration is anything but the heaven on earth that the youthful billionaires of the Electronics Age would have it be. More accurately, this callow world is a fool's paradise, best christened Absurdia.

Donald Trump

Shocking Election, Rude Awakening, Rare Opportunity
Buckle up! The post-election winds of change will soon begin to blow. Trumpism will soon sweep across the land. A better or worse America is in the offing. All depends upon President-elect Donald Trump: a highly perplexing eccentric, an opinionated and brazenly brash operator, a conceited, dramatic buffoon, a very capable risk-taking corporate-world executive, and an untried politician. Should Trump

remain the questionable blunderbuss he was during the presidential campaign, America will surely go from bad to worse. On the other hand, should it dawn upon Trump that his personal interests have to become secondary to America's general welfare—and this is definitely possible—America is just as likely to go from bad to better. It remains to be seen how many-sided Trump can be!

In the meantime, America is left deeply apprehensive about the campaigner Trump's candid views and bluntly proclaimed intentions, and for good reason: Much that in America is generally accepted or even treasured is jeopardized, and much that Trump would initiate is commonly deemed appalling.

Trump would loose the hungry hound of change. He would act quickly and legislate decisively, and would have recourse to whatever measures or tactics he deemed necessary to make America great again.

To this end, Trump would immediately focus critically on those world-trade agreements that he considered detrimental to America's well-being. The Trans-Pacific Trade Partnership (2016), President Obama's free-trade agreement with some eleven Pacific Rim countries, would be renegotiated or terminated, as would the North Atlantic Free Trade Agreement (1994) with Mexico and Canada. Irked by China's veritable flood of state-subsidized imports to America and very troubled by the resultant negative impact on American firms and workers, Trump would quickly inflict a punitive remedial tariff on all Chinese imports. Undocumented Mexican immigrants would be summarily deported, a wall would be built to keep would-be Mexican immigrants out of the country, and for security reasons, foreign Muslims would be barred from America, and all American Muslims would be registered. To better contain a chronically militant Iran, Trump would forthwith dismantle America's too lenient nuclear accord (2015) with the country, and to end the world's half-hearted sputtering military engagement with Isis, Trump would have America's military might boldly take on and annihilate the fanatical Islamic autocracy. And NATO would quickly have to learn to manage its affairs without America's long-time military and financial aid.

Joseph Mileck

The foremost threats and promises of Trump's campaign domestic policy were no less forthright than those of his campaign foreign policy. To enhance America's wanting healthcare, President Trump would immediately repeal The Affordable Care Act (2010), a.k.a Obamacare. And in emulation of the Western World's industrialized countries, he would guarantee better care for America's elderly and a six-week paid maternity leave for all American mothers. Persuaded that climate change is a hoax, Trump would quickly dismantle President Obama's environmental regulations, and little concerned about the global level of carbon dioxide emissions, would promptly lift all restrictions on coal and oil use, and would even threaten to turn America's back on the Paris Pact (2015) and its international efforts to stem Earth's alleged warming. To enhance a flagging American economy, Trump would repatriate corporate profits deliberately stashed abroad (some 2 trillion dollars), to avoid an onerous 35 percent corporate tax, and he would manage this by reducing the corporate tax on profits housed abroad to but 10 percent. This tax windfall will boost America's infrastructure spending and thereby bolstering its ever-dwindling workforce. A later, standing 15 percent corporate tax on all corporation profits would suffice to stabilize America's ever fluctuating economy.

A successful businessman's belated determination to make his seriously-fractured and faltering country great again, has occasioned a bitter national uproar. Trump's failure to expound upon his very contentious and but curtly expressed priorities—his failure to provide any telling details about this purpose, implementation and possible untoward consequences—left both Republicans and Democrats infuriated and with no alternative but to become bitterly *ad hominem* in their reaction.

An irate splintered and very troubled America began promptly to dispose of Trump in no uncertain terms, and America has to date continued to do so unremittingly. Publicly, one of America's leading real estate tycoons became a xenophobe, homophobe, and Islamaphobe, an uncouth salesman, an inveterate liar, *et al.* These nasty epithets notwithstanding, America's electorate chose to make Trump its president, and for a good, though not immediately apparent reason.

To consider America's perplexing election of Trump nothing but an absurd aberration, as has commonly been done, is simplistic and inadequate explanation. More plausible, America's low opinion of Trump was primarily an unambiguous rejection of his person, and the electorate's choice of Trump was not an approval of Trump, but of his loudly trumpeted determination to change America for the better. Deep down, many Americans, both Republicans and Democrats, hoped desperately and perhaps even believed that Trump, highly successful pragmatic businessman that he was, would be an equally successful *realpolitiker*, and could indeed change America for the better. America was simply a seriously fractured and deeply troubled country desperately intent upon change, and any change could be for the better.

By way of summary: America's low opinion of Trump was and still is primarily a brusque rejection of his person and not of his little known sweeping political intents. Similarly, the electorate's choice of Trump was not an approval of Trump, but of his determination to make America great again. Many Americans hoped that Trump the pragmatist would modify his brazen ill-considered policy appropriately enough to usher in a new great America.

Change has become America's order of the day. A country in disarray is in dire need of change, an angry citizenry expects change, and president-elect Trump is planning widespread change. A propitious juncture in America's history, one rife with possibilities, both good and bad.

But Americans will first have to better themselves, before America can be changed for the better. The public at large will have to become more informed, more reflective and more involved in matters social, political, economic and cultural; the gridlock in Washington and the corporate world's manipulation of Congress will have to be scotched; and America's very troubling financial, racial and religious divides will have to be bridged.

The betterment of America will depend no less upon Trump himself: upon a mellowing of his cantankerous person and upon a moderation of his drastic political intents. Just to dismiss Trump as a reckless buffoon, brash operator or a novice politician lacking all presidential qualifications, would only cause him to bristle and persuade him to continue to operate in his usual imperious manner, and any constructive interaction between president and public in pending changes in America's medical care, education, immigration, trade, and outsourcing of jobs and industries, would be negligible.

More broadly, if America is to be changed for the better, its treasured materialism, rank consumerism, unfettered individualism and unbridled capitalism will also have to be sensitively moderated.

Finally, if his mission to make America great again is not to become an embarrassing fiasco, President-elect Trump will quickly have to become appropriately open-minded, well-meaning, duly informed and patiently persistent. Private interest will also have to yield to the common good. Furthermore, Trump would also be well-advised: to acquaint himself thoroughly and sympathetically with the general needs and wants of the American people; to steep himself as quickly as possible in both domestic matters and foreign affairs; to cultivate a good working relationship with Congress; to surround himself with knowledgeable and practised counselors; and to endeavor to become something of an idealist-pragmatist.

A Country Perched for Change

A fractured America is overdue for change.
Its angry people are demanding change,
And President Trump is championing change.
Will change take place?
Hope is high,
Time will tell!
(December 11, 2016)

A MISCELLANY
OF
TOPICAL ASIDES

(essay) a loose sally of the mind.

(Samuel Johnson)

Adam and Eve

*I*t was only with Adam and Eve, the garden of paradise and the apple, that we humans became what we are, blessed and cursed by the power of discriminating thought. We have, ever since, been laboring under the burden of thought, our original sin. This is our existential lot. With thought came awareness of good and evil and the accompanying agony. More significant, this godly trait that separates us from animals brought with it the more agonizing awareness of death.

Ever since, the faculty of thought, the source of our awareness of death, has been used in a vain effort to battle death, to blot it out, to overcome it. Paradoxically civilization and culture are the fruits of this futile losing battle.

The Natural and the Moral

*T*o lie and to cheat, to covet and to steal, to hate and to kill, all natural impulses intent upon survival, are curbed by morality but never eradicated. They serve raw life no less than moral impulses serve civilized life. Life at large is an interplay of the natural and of the moral. Both will and must be served.

Our "There"

*N*either the "there" from which we all once came,
Nor the "there" to which we all once repair
Is a "there."
We alone, the conscious something between two voids,
And our consciousness of self and others, of things and voids, are our only reality
Our only "there."

American Universities

*U*niversities in America began to become industrial complexes in their size and structure soon after the Second World War. By the seventies, the commercialization of the new industrial complexes had become the latest trend in the transformation of the traditional university. All of this has been accompanied by a gradual erosion of education by general fragmentation, by growing friction in the ranks of the faculty, spreading indifference to students and financial corruption. Should this trend continue, the American university is likely to become a business corporation, and education, a money-making commodity.

The Annual Convention of the Modern Language Association

*T*he literati of the MLA gather in solemn session once a year to pontificate and to be seen. Hotel lobby and lecture rooms accommodate pinch-lipped paunchy men sporting bushy beards and turtleneck sweaters, and smiling amazons in high-laced boots. This entourage of apostles of literature differs little from year to year. Indeed, the annual event has become a gathering of familiar faces, briefcases and academic civility.

Subjects under discussion in room upon room range impressively and the deluge of presentation titles are exciting in their promise, and this is so from year to year. And every year is very much a disappointing *déjà vu*. The politically engaged among the program participants are characteristically more politics than literature, the apostles of methodology are characteristically more theory than literature, and the authentic students of literature are characteristically profound beyond comprehension. Listener reactions are also quite characteristic from year to year. Some pose abstruse questions and more to impress than to extend argument, others squirm in boredom and discomfort, and still others assume intelligent frozen faces while quite asleep. And this charade has gone on for almost a hundred years. Literature deserves better!

Christianity

Christianity has all but ceased to be a religion. It has, by and large, become either a sociohistorical interest or an aesthetic experience, or a matter of indifference. God has become a figment of the imagination, the Bible but literature, religious ritual but drama, religious music and song but secularized pleasure, cathedrals but architectural mementoes, and the ten commandments but moral fossils. What on our cultural landscape was once a spiritual inspiration, moral guide and solace has become tolerated anomaly, academic curiosity, or but a dispensable nuisance.

The Paradox of Life

Heaven and hell—
And every religion has had its
Variations on these themes—
Are humanity's greatest figment
Of the imagination,
Are indeed palliatives and placebos,
But what magnificent fictive realities!
For it is not by bread alone that we live,
But by the fear and hope
Inspired by the non-existent.
The paradox of life!

Hyperbole

*N*ewspaper reports are leavened by hyperbole.
To "give up" is pedestrian, "abandon" has flare!
To "promise" is ordinary, to "vow" is lofty!
To "defeat" is casual, to "vanquish" is dramatic!
To "persuade" is anaemic, to "convince" is vigorous!
Hyperbole, to be sure, adds a touch of panache, but only at the expense of a dash of truth!

Modern Literary Study

*L*iterary scholarship has become fragmentized cultural philosophy expressed in esoteric terminologies and resulting in a cacophonous Babel babble. All this cerebral sophistication is not the zenith but the nadir of modern literary study.

Irony

*B*eyond its deceptively playful offense and its titillating verbal display,
The ironist's irony is an effective antidepressant and an unmistakable lash,
A means whereby the ironist can make comment of attack and equanimity of agitation.
A dual purpose is deviously served!

Rock Music

*R*ock music is musical insanity. It was born of hatred and fed on sex, is dependent upon drugs and preaches a phony brotherhood.

Rock music is barbarism gone berserk, gutter music rotten at its core and plied by hypocritical buffoons who laugh all the way to the bank. Its days are numbered!

Make Believe

Truths, beliefs, values are only personal, social or cultural decisions. Arbitrary or even capricious though these decisions are, personal, social and cultural well-being are dependent upon them and their fictional absoluteness.

Make believe is a necessary, indeed, inherent part of human life.

How Humans Cope

Philosophies are rationalizations that try to account for the unaccountable,

Religions are palliatives that try to make bearable the unbearable,

Moralities are constraints to keep in line,

And ideals are a spur to ennoble.

This is how humans have learned to cope with life!

The Plight of the Jews

The diaspora and Zionism, once the reference points for Jewry, have been displaced by the Holocaust, and it is paying off in greater attention and sympathy attracted.

The Holocaust was both a calamity beyond compare and a blessing in disguise. It exterminated Jews by the millions, and it provided world-wide impetus and direction to Zionism's reawakened Jewish consciousness.

Art

*A*rt is actuality: actuality mirrored, expanded, satirized, rendered comic or tragic, mimicked, distorted, gilded, hyperbolized, fantasized, romanticized, idealized, ironicized, celebrated and denigrated. Art is actuality altered by the artist's imprint or enveloped by the artist's shadow.

Art is personal even when impersonal

And universal even when personal!

Idealists

*L*ike Hamlet long ago, most of our passionate idealists today are of the persuasion that the world is out of joint. For them, neither their fellow humans nor the world are what they could or should be. But does this fault lie just out there? Perhaps the so-persuaded idealist is himself not up to snuff. Perhaps he is too acutely aware of the mote in his brother's eye to behold the beam in his own! Perhaps his own little world is not exactly in order! Perhaps his negative view of his fellow men and the world at large is, in part or even basically, a projected criticism of himself and his! To fault only fellow humans and the world is to fault too little!

The Camera

*T*he ubiquitous camera is becoming the prime marauding intruder of the 20th century. It has become an eye that nothing escapes. Nothing is private for it, nothing is profane, nothing is beyond propriety and all must be exposed to view, to inform the public, sate its curiosity and amuse it. Thanks to the camera and its adjunct cinema and television, ours has become a panoramic view that little escapes.

Almost everything from visually sublime to the visually ridiculous is at our eye's disposal: from private bedrooms to public play fields, from drawing room to houses of ill repute, from execution chambers to legislature in session, from the poor on the streets to the wealthy in their mansions, from Shakespeare to talk shows, from beauty pageants to quiz shows, from ballroom to outdoors, from symphony hall to noisy mobs, from courtroom to bathroom. And as most things in life, this visual feast is both bane and blessing. It surely leaves us broadly informed and thoroughly entertained, but in becoming paramount in our preoccupations, has thrust substance and thought into the background.

A balance of outer and the inner would be more salutary for both culture and individual!

Less eye candy and more brain-food!

Relativity

Relativity does not mean that nothing is right and that nothing is wrong, and that everything goes. Right and wrong are not cancelled, only rendered relative. Relativity does not afford license, it demands even greater self-discipline than do absolutes. Relative truths must be lived as though absolute. That is a real challenge!

A Split Personality

"Every" man is both a "natural" and a "civilized" self, a split personality, two disparate halves at cross-purposes. Though he dreams up his religions and his moralities, he keeps on behaving in the manner of his "natural" self. Religions and morality gainsay his instincts and are a violation of his "natural" inclinations. This is "every" man's curse and his glory. To this vital split he can attribute all he has ever accomplished, and to this split he also owes most of his suffering.

Emotions Have Usurped Reason

The sober views of those who are not immediately involved and have nothing at stake have little appeal in our turbulent world. Painful experience and emotional agony speak more loudly and know better. One must only be a victim and agonize to become an authority.

Today's wisdom derives reflexively from direct experience and suffering: One must be a teacher to criticize an educational system, a black to teach blacks effectively, a victim to be able to appreciate violence and to counter it appropriately, and one must have suffered a sickness to know that sickness and know how best to heal it.

Ageless wisdom born of disinterested reflection on life, its joys and agonies, has become passé. Direct experience and accompanying joy or pain have made instant experts of all of us. Emotions have usurped reason!

The Whole and the Part

America spells confrontation not cooperation,
Polarization more than integration,
Raptor capitalism and feeble socialism.
Here management both proposes and disposes,
Here workers fight for more income and less effort,
Here the whole is sacrificed for the part,
And eventually whole and part will fall apart.
For this socio-economic world there is no grand future!

Free Trade

Free trade will not be the international blessing it is touted to be. The bigger, the economically stronger, the greater the advantage. International capitalism, with no holds barred, is sure to run amuck.

For their increased imports, poor third-world countries are likely to
overgraze their land, strip their forests, and leave their waters fishless.
Nineteenth-century political imperialism has gone its way,
Twenty-first century economic imperialism will soon hold sway,
And the business world will have its day!

Belief and Disbelief

All our truths, all our beliefs, all our values, like all our laws are but
part of a social contract. All are absolute in terms of the whole, and all
are relative beyond that whole. Belief is the binding adhesive of this
social contract, and disbelief the solvent that will unglue the whole.
What has come together will in due time fall apart. All moves from
belief to disbelief, from formation to dissolution, from life to death.
And then the reverse begins!

Our Waning Culture

Too much that is negative is simply ascribed to material poverty,
Too little to our Western World's growing poverty of belief and values.
Ours is less a social problem than a cultural illness.
Our old culture is dying and a new has yet to be born.
We are the blighted, fated to experience
Both the agony of death and the pain of birth!

Americans

There is no *American*, there are only many kinds of Americans.
America is not a being but a becoming.
And this will not change until the country ceases to hold
An attraction for the world's many hopeful emigrants.

And this is not likely soon,
And perhaps should never happen.

Buzzword Banners

*M*ulticulturalism and pluralism can easily degenerate into multi-garbage anarchy.
These are buzzword banners
Waved enthusiastically by politicians fishing for supportive unwary constituents,
Or pie-in-the-sky theories
Argued just as enthusiastically and blindly by ivory-tower intellectuals.
Political gain for one camp, intellectual sport for the other!
And an inevitable loss for the country at large.
Politicians are too pragmatic and intellectuals too unrealistic.

Convictions

*T*he realist: the road of actuality leads to life,
The romantic: the road of dreams leads to bliss,
The moralist: the road of virtue leads to heaven,
The hedonist: the road of pleasure leads to satisfaction,
The skeptic: the road of belief leads to disbelief,
The agnostic: the road of know not leads to wise detachment,
The cynic: the road of selfishness is the road of life,
The nihilist: the road to anywhere leads nowhere!

Truths

*S*cientific truths evolve and this is the strength of the sciences,
Religious truths are static and this is the strength of religions.

Essayistic Ventures and Topical Asides

Unfortunately, each camp has always been prone to argue its infallibility.
The reach of each is shorter than the grasp.
How very human!

Cemeteries

Cemeteries are the past etched in stone,
Blood, flesh, and bones become ash, dirt, and memory.
Precious residues!

Television

At its worst—and it's rarely otherwise—
Television pollutes the mind and dulls the emotions,
And undoubtedly lethargizes mentally and physically.
At its best—and these are rare moments indeed—
Television informs, excites and energizes.
On balance, television has clearly exacted too much,
And has to date just as clearly afforded too little!
A paradox of which telly buffs are happily oblivious!

What we Need

We need more wisdom and not more knowledge,
More green paths than highways of information.
More humanity and not more technology.
Unfortunately there is little likelihood
That East or West will soon choose
To get off its electronics' roller-coaster.
Robotsville promises to become our heaven/hell!

The Ideal and the Real

The rare and fortunate human being is that person whose feet are firmly planted on earth and whose head hovers above the clouds. Such a person is at home both in the abstract world of language and thought and in the concrete world of things, action and interaction. This is an ideal human possibility!
The common and unfortunate human being is that person with both feet and head either above the clouds or on earth. This is a prevalent human actuality!

Cultural Decline

Technologically we are in seventh heaven,
Spiritually we are adrift and foundering.
Technologists are blindly euphoric,
Thinkers are blindly distressed,
Laymen are blindly indifferent,
And cultural collapse is imminent.

Deconstruction

Our cultural realities have already become banalities!
Lies have become more profitable than truth,
Actuality is rapidly yielding to virtual reality,
Personality has taken precedence over character,
Stars of whatever ilk have become our models of choice,
Living has become frenzied activity, relationships flimsy attachments,
What once was constructed is now systematically deconstructed,
Relativity prevails where fixed values once guided.
Hectic becoming has become our being,
A culture spent, waiting to be replaced!

How the Winds Blow

The 20th-century is world-wide hell-bound on shattering all restraints,
Traditional cultural values, religious beliefs, social practices, laws and
moralities have become prisons.
A long creative becoming has become a raucous dissolution,
Back with reckless abandon to history's primitive morass.
Deconstruction is the rallying cry,
Anarchic freedom the passion, and wayward destruction the inevitable result!

Social Cluster

Jews, Blacks, Hispanics, homosexuals and social clusters of whatever ilk,
Should not segregate themselves.
Just as surely, society at large should not segregate itself.
Neither camp can afford this luxury morally, economically or politically.
Commonality and not difference should determine our relationships.
We are all humans, a simple truth forgotten too easily,
And for questionable advantage!

Success

Success is an opinion not an absolute,
A moment, not an eternity,
Not salvation, only a touch of grace,
Something to be savored, not devoured.

Religion

*R*eligion has descended from its erstwhile ethereal, other-worldly spirituality,
The material world has become our heavenly sphere.
We now worship in the church of business and feast at the altar of consumption.
We are becoming what we consume and becoming just as dispensable.
God is dead and Mammon prevails!
For better or for worse?

Imperialism

*I*n its new-found megalomania,
America would dictate to the world politically,
Exploit the world economically
And convert the world morally.
What puerile hubris!
What inane imperialism!

Newscasting

*N*ewscasting has become a very profitable entertainment industry. Theater sells! News has become exciting serial entertainment, a daily time-filler. Like so much else in the USA, newscasting has been thoroughly hollywoodized. The simple pine tree has become decked out Christmas tree. Actuality has yielded to profitable virtuality. Newscasting has become but another of our many sources of titillating diversion.

Psychology

The psychology industry has experienced a long due revival!
It feeds off human misfortune as ravenously as vultures feed on carrion.
Its trauma experts and long-term grief counselors dispense their fast-soul-food with abandon and no more responsibly than McDonalds its fast-stomach-food. And in both cases the results are questionable.

Chance

The chance of life is the spice of life,
No one escapes its sweet or bitter sweep.
It gives or takes, brings together or tears apart
And it knows no favorites.
However, chance, like a loose cannon, is anything but random!
Nothing is beyond cause and effect,
But ultimate cause and effect are discernible only to God!

Interaction

If interaction is to be positive,
Don't overwhelm, persuade,
Talk less and listen more,
Empathize, don't antagonize,
Whisper don't shout,
Help rather than harm,
Be neither arrogant nor servile,
And tranquil rather than agitated.
You will then be heeded and valued!
What more do you want?

The Individual

*I*t is rare for a person at odds with himself or herself to be content with society and life at large. The former almost inevitably colors the latter, indeed the latter generally mirrors the former. Not to come to grips and to terms with the self precludes coming to grips and to terms with society and with life. All literally begins and ends with the self. Each individual's lot is essentially of his or her own making, ergo, of his or her own choosing.

To Shape and to be Reshaped

*L*iteracy was once an education's focal concern.
The concept has now been qualified to suit technology's needs.
Literacy's verbal skills have yielded to digital literacy's computer skills,
The former intent upon human growth,
The latter more intent upon human function.
The computer is rapidly reshaping its inventors,
A phenomenon as old as the hills!
We have always been shaped by the very things we shape.

Forgiveness

*N*o wrong once done can be undone! Remorse, penance and efforts to amend should follow. Never again! If so, the anger of the wronged may or will abate. To expect forgiveness is to expect an unmerited reward. A wrong that leads to a reward invites repetition. Wrongs and their forgiveness twice reward the sinner. The unfortunate cycle is likely to repeat itself. A *mea culpa,* individual or collective, expecting forgiveness is a tainted confession. It undoes nothing! No wrong once done can be undone! We cannot and should not forget, nor do we have the moral obligation or moral right to forgive. Not forgiveness, but acceptance should follow due remorse and due amendment: acceptance of the changed!

Entertainment

The USA has become a vast entertainment world!
Entertainment, not drugs, has become our major addiction.
Our wealth of entertainment possibility has become extended
From the theater and concert hall, the sports field and news media,
Politics and soap operas to weather reports, advertising
And even to the courtroom.
All is fun!
Means and matter may well become exhausted
Before we become jaded and return to moderation and sobriety.
Time will tell!

The Holocaust

The Holocaust must never be forgotten,
A horrible tragedy suffered by the Jews!
But it should also not become a victim's
Timeless lament for racial or political advantage.
In time, it must become a powerful metaphor
For man's inhumanity to his fellow man,
For the frailty of culture and civilization,
Indeed for life itself at its worst,
Particular implication become universal.
A powerful lesson for mankind!

Science

Mankind must have its mythologies,
Science its latest!
Mythologies speak their metaphorical truths,
Science does no more!

Science is almost pathologically snoopy,
Its nosiness is arrogantly prosaic,
Its truths are as dated as astounding,
It epitomizes the hubris of mankind,
Reflects our controlled uncreative best.
Its doing is but an undoing,
And its quest will remain in vain.
We are but mortals and not Gods,
Something science chooses to forget,
As it toils in God's vineyards.

Nirvana

Discontent is fertile soil for anger and hostility,
On the other hand, content spawns affability and love.
To counter the former,
And to foster the latter,
Stop willing and wanting,
Breath slowly and deeply,
And nirvana is yours!
Or so Buddha would argue.

Cultural Plight

Our old Gods are gone, our old myths are spent, and our old values
are dead,
And our modern world is changing too quickly and too radically
For new Gods to be born, new myths to germinate and new values
to spread.
We have become a ship without a rudder in a very stormy sea!

Flux

The intellectual world knows no terra firma.
All is shifting sands.
The beliefs of the past are revised or cast aside by the quests of the
present, the truths of which, in turn, yield to the novelties of the future.
Being is but a blip in a perpetually roiling becoming.
Sic transit gloria mentis!

The Servants of God

I doubt that it was at the behest of our omnipotent, omnipresent and
omniscient God that our Christian crusaders undertook to liberate
Jerusalem from the Mideast infidels, that the Grand Inquisitors
destroyed the bodies to save the souls of obdurate heretics, that Bush
our warrior-president unleashed the dogs of war to spread God's gift
of freedom to mankind throughout the world.
There has never been a dearth of self-appointed and self-anointed
servants of God!

Language and War

General Sanchez approved a "stress matrix" in the interrogation of Iraqi prisoners of war.

What is the arcane phrase "stress matrix" but verbal camouflage for "illegal inhumane abuse," a violation of the Geneva Convention.

Language is one of the first victims of war.

It then, paradoxically, becomes an instrument of war!

The Boon and the Blight of Television

Of our media, television has become paramount!

Our world of entertainment revolves around television!

Solace is now a ready commodity, aloneness a thing of the past,

And vicarious action and ready information bountiful.

Television has become our common commodity, our society's binding adhesive.

A daily bounteous fare, it has also become our veiled affliction, a narcotic addiction, our virtual reality,

And no longer just a potential Big Brother brain-washing control!

The Celebrated and the Ordinary

Ours is a celebrity culture:

We lionize the notorious,

Canonize the stars of entertainment,

Aggrandize the heroes of sportland,

And idolize the tycoons of technology.

The ordinary is too little, too common and too boring—

Clearly not worthy of note!

Blood Cousins

Scratch a saint and a sinner will wince,
Scratch a cynic and an idealist will bleed.
The extremes appear to be blood cousins!

Exceptionalism

America's blatant belief in its exceptionalism did not begin with G. W. Bush. Kennedy and Wilson before Bush and Th. Roosevelt before and F. Roosevelt after Wilson were no less persuaded. And Americans as a whole share in this hubris.

Nor is this a peculiarly American phenomenon. All past empires were born of and eventually undone by this passion. America's fall will not be an exception!

Fanaticism

Bush and his entourage are passionate apostles of belief!
Belief dictates their every action.
Contrary facts are brazenly modified or ignored,
Desired results justify the worst of means.
Convictions of whatever ilk unfettered are nothing more than fanaticism,
And fanaticism has always done more damage than good!

America and I

In my acrid view of the reality that is America, I am intent upon being honest and fair as possible, am despairing and plaintively hopeful, and am both angry and sad. Fellow spirits will nod in agreement, but most others are likely to dispose of my pronunciamentos as absurd, irrelevant and unpatriotic, the ramblings of a misguided self-righteous and sanctimonious moralist. That I may be such an idealist and moralist does not diminish the veracity of my observations!

Cultural Fingerprints

The imprint of painting, sculpture and architecture—Leonardo da Vinci, Michelangelo, Titian, Raphael, Brunelleschi, Fra Filippo Lippi, Botticelli, Bellini, Tintoretto, Veronese, Donatello, Ghiberti *et al.*—characterizes Renaissance Italy.

Will America of the 21st-century be remembered primarily for its Wal Mart, Kmart, Staples, Home Depot, Costco, Toys R Us, its Wendy's, Burger King, McDonalds and its multitudinous supermarkets and sundry megastores?

Aloneness and Loneliness

Aloneness is a circumstance of the outer world,
Loneliness is an affliction of the inner world.
The former is a choice, the latter is lot!

According to the Gospel of our Born-Again Evangelicals

Ours is the best of all democracies, indeed a world divinely blessed. Our leader has a messianic mission to endow the world with our democracy and liberty, and if need be, to kill and destroy to realize his mission. We are God's chosen servants and can therefore do no wrong. And all this is but a prologue to Armageddon, the final battle between the forces of good and evil.

A dangerous mix of religiosity, politics and delusion!

Essayistic Ventures and Topical Asides

The Battered and the Abusive

In the media, the adjective "battered" all too commonly accompanies the noun "women," and the adjective "abusive" is no less frequently affixed to the noun "men." This featured characterization of the "man/woman" relationship can only exacerbate the traditional "battle of the sexes," itself a questionably hyperbolized slogan.

Private Enterprise

*P*rivate enterprise is not always the cure that the American business world have it to be! Medical care in America would exemplify this. Our highly touted medical care is the most expensive, the most disorganized and the most error prone in the industrialized Western World. To be sure, while the care for the many is wanting, the care for the wealthy is the best in the world!

Paradox

*T*hanks to the ease of modern travel, we can readily cultivate our continental and global contacts, but human intimacy has only become rarer and separateness more acute.

Thanks to the wonders of modern technological communication isolation is breeched as never before, yet we find ourselves disconnected and alone as never before.

We have become nomads with many tents, well-acquainted with the far reaches of our country and of the world, yet we are homeless and stranger to one another.

What promised greater togetherness has paradoxically fostered greater aloneness! We seem not to fear aloneness enough to cultivate togetherness, and distance seems to be less threatening than intimacy.

Children and Education

To put an academic halter on pre-kindergarten children, even upon kindergartners, is to stimulate cognitive skills and to hamper emotional growth and social aptitudes. This trend in elementary school education will inevitably turn out more academic achievers who are even more emotionally troubled and socially lame than the "geeks" our schools now breed. It is by far better that the adult world and its pressing academic interests be imposed later than sooner upon the child world. Children twisted out of emotional shape and left wanting socially, become emotionally troubled adults and social misfits. We already have enough of these distortions! Better that our elementary educational institutions focus more upon balancing of emotional, social and academic growth.

A Reversion

Our Christmas holidays have to an alarming degree reverted to their pagan origin. Saturnalia was for the Romans a week of drunken revelry, sexual promiscuity and lawlessness, and for Americans Christmas has become a hiatus of hectic excesses, a manic rush and a carnival of noisy commercialism. To date, we have only been spared Rome's bawdy songs, naked dancing and human sacrifice!

Obligation and Freedom

The pronoun *we* dominates in the world of business.
The pronoun *I* dominates in the university world.
In the business world, the group, the *we*, has the obligation to serve business to its advantage.
In the world of the university, the individual, the *I*, has the freedom to advance his field of expertise in whatever way he chooses.
Obligation and freedom have their separate purview and serve their separate purposes!

We, the Programmed

We are all programmed both to a comforting and a disquieting degree, and both are to good advantage and to serious disadvantage. Structured living, patterned behavior and organized thought are rewards for the ordinary many and the whole! Confinement, restriction and stultification is the price paid by the exceptional few!

It is Time

Violence has had its day, a long and dismal stay.
It has served its futile purpose and soon must go its way.
Peaceful accommodation must at some future time
Be our guiding hope and *modus operandi!*
Else continuous world slaughter will become our *modus vivendi!*

An Enigma

America is an enigmatic colossus, a blend of humanitarianism and militarism, a Dr. Jekyll and Mr. Hyde, and Mr. Hyde is becoming dominant! And yet America would argue exceptionalism, would be a beacon of morality and a democracy to be emulated.
An enigma indeed!

A Dilemma

Our ever-increasing recourse to antibiotics has become an ever-increasing necessity and a constant failure since bacteria, in self-defense, ever mutate.
We are on a brakeless rollercoaster! We began something we cannot stop without tragic results.

C'est la vie!
Life has no ultimate solutions.
Each solution spawns yet another problem!

Tilting at Windmills

*T*he problem of 11 million illegal immigrants in the U.S.A. may be more blessing than problem. But for these illegals, thousands of American businesses would fail, and but for these immigrants, millions of their dependents in Mexico would suffer want. Both the country left and the country entered are by and large the better for this northern migration. Spawned by Mexican poverty and fueled by American need, this migration was and is inevitability and less a problem than but a problematic blessing!

In their present obsession with illegal immigrants, our quixotic legislators are but tilting at the windmill. Too much political ado about too little social need!

Brazen Pose

*T*he USA is not an exceptional nation, but one of many. America's history is not unique, but only a part of world history. And our ventures abroad are not driven by a pious passion to spread democracy and liberty, but by an imperialist lusting for political and economic power. Ignorance, conceit and lies know no bounds!

Self-interest and Common Good

*A*merica's neo-conservatives, passionately committed to radical individualism on the personal, corporate and national plane, have become alarmingly indifferent to the common good, both social and international. Theirs is a myopic "either-or."

But self-interest and common good are a polar "either-or" only in their extremes. In moderation, both possibilities could be adequately served. This compromise could shrink the presently growing chasm between our many who have too little and our few who have too much, and could reduce the number of such devastating misadventures as Afghanistan and Iraq. But intelligent and human compromise in America is short in supply!

A Buffeted Colossus

*A*merica is an enigma that both attracts and repels. Its radical individualism, exceptionalism and narcissism, its intense religiosity, nationalism and arrogance, its lack of self-examination, only tentative respect for other countries and its wealth, its power, liberty and democracy have long attracted the love, admiration, envy, suspicion and distrust of the world at large. This admixture of conflicting responses became unambiguous hostility with America's misadventures in Afghanistan and Iraq. America's long-time and unwavering support of Israel's decimation of the Palestinian people has acutely intensified this hostility. This hardly bodes well!

Patriotism and Wars

*D*emocracy, liberty and justice should be spread by the force of law and not by the law of force, namely the military. America's military forces have characteristically been used not to defend America but to attack its enemies. To die in defense of America can be deemed laudably patriotic. To kill for an aggressive America on the warpath is madness, sick patriotism!

The Terrible Isms

*A*merica's *triumphalism* is grating foe and friend alike. It will have its way or cease to play.

An arrogant and doomed *unilateralism* characterizes America's foreign policy.

America's self-righteous crusade to remake the world after its own image is *imperialism* in an obvious disguise.

Terrorism is President Bush's excuse for his abuse of power.

And his messianic *exceptionalism* and religious *patriotism* are reminiscent of Adolf Hitler's absurd *Aryanism* and disastrous fatherland gospel!

The Exceptional or the Exemplary

*S*hould exceptionalism determine America's international role, or should it be exemplariness?

Exceptionalism gives license to itself, exemplariness imposes responsibility upon itself.

Exceptionalism breeds inequity and imperialism, exemplariness fosters equality and democracy.

Exceptionalism leads to world strife, exemplariness advances peaceful co-existence. The disastrous results of exceptionalism of Bush's America were inevitable. A change of course is overdue!

A Fact of Life

*W*e humans are no less different above than below the shoulders.

Evolution above and below the shoulders determines cultures and their evolution.

We humans are no more equal above than below the shoulders.

People and peoples are different, not equal.

We must accept differences and resolve them and stop our futile academic argument of equality!

Notwithstanding, equal rights, privileges and responsibility must be accorded to all, if only to assure a reasonably peaceful society.

Ignorance is Bliss

*L*eft to its own devices, ignorance spawns apathy. In times of relative tranquility, the apathy of the many gives free rein to the unscrupulous empowered few.

Exploited by merchants of fear, ignorance can easily fall prey to hysteria and hysteria permits ideologues to pursue unhampered their nefarious purposes, among them, war.

Yes, ignorance of the many is indeed bliss for the few!

Religion and Politics

*R*eligion and politics are a bad mix. Each becomes corrupt and each pollutes the other.

When religions in their extreme and politics in their extreme co-mix, the results can be devastating: inevitable wars.

The Christian West and the Islamic East have succumbed to this mixture, and the world is the worst for it!

Aloneness

*I*ronically, the more sophisticated our modes of electronic communications become, the more separated and disconnected we become.

When physical interaction and accompanying conversation are replaced by remote contact and telegrammic messaging, friendships become contacts and aloneness our fate.

Genius may blossom in aloneness, the many wither!

Countries that run Amuck

*A*ny country that believes it can remake the world after its own image is both naïve and blind to history.

Any country that argues exceptionalism is indulging in self-delusion.

Any country that insists upon exclusive possession of weapons of mass destruction is anything but mindful of the welfare of the world at large.

Any country obsessively intent upon absolute security is a country forever engaged in war.

Any country led by a leader with a messianic mission is a country hell-bent.

There always have been countries in this wrong,
America has of late joined the throng!

I, Others and Fate

*E*motionally, I am beneficiary and/or victim of my own expectations, of the expectations of others, and of the caprice of fate. I can do little about others and even less about fate, but I can do much about myself. I can be my own fate. Indeed, I am my own fate, willingly or unwillingly, actively or passively! "Seize self-fate by the forelock" is a good guiding adage! Try it, you may like it!

American Democracy

*A*merican democracy, like every viable human institution, has, from its inception, never ceased to change. Becoming is its being and change is its salvation. Dictatorships, in contrast, are static and doomed. They do not change, they break!

American democracy has by and large been changing for the worst since the Second World War. However, there is some reason to believe that Americans will soon have their fill of this change and will hopefully opt for a democracy less arrogant and less intent upon power and empire, and more understanding and more appreciative and acceptant of the different.

Our Blissful Existential Agony

*E*very living being, wittingly or unwittingly, is caught in an existential plight. A being is life incarnate and life's blind passion is to sustain itself. A being is also an individual entity tormented by its essential separateness and resultant aloneness and obsessed by an instinctual longing for togetherness, for escape from its basic separateness, the very essence of individual life.

Would that we could have our cake and eat it too!

Only in death does this instinctual tug of irrational energies end!

A Questionable Drift in Focus

*W*hen we become knowledgeable, given to the arts and sciences, we do so in the hope that we will resultantly be better prepared for life. Such was the persuasion of the philosopher-poet Goethe. This is no less true in the 21st century than it was in the 18th except for a different understanding of "prepared for life." Goethe's was an existential concern while ours is a social matter: position, money and power. A philosophical 18th century and a pragmatic 21st century!

Groups and Consequences

*T*here are the relatively pure thinkers and the relatively pure feelers, and between these disparate groups, the equally disparate feeling thinkers and the thinking feelers. The interaction of these clusters is characterized by an appalling lack of understanding and/or appreciation of the other.

Joseph Mileck 177

Then there are the racial, ethnic, religious, cultural, gender, sex, age and professional groups. Here, too, mutual understanding and appreciation are a rarity. Little wonder that strife characterizes the human family!

Wars

Wars have always been initiated for good causes and/or moral reasons: to guarantee security, to combat evil, to defend the faith, to spread democracy and liberty, to promote peace etc. Furthermore, the enemy is always to blame: power hungry, a threat to peace, a political threat etc. All this is but inspirational window dressing to justify a questionable undertaking and to persuade the gullible many to cooperate.

G. W. Bush's reasons for waging war (security, democracy, liberty) are old hat, nothing but repetition of traditional excuses. And what really motivated Bush & Co. (political and economic power) was just as traditional. Berthold Brecht's bald dismissal of war as but a continuation of business by other means, rings truer than Bush's lame excuse for war.

Poets cut to the quick,
Politicians dance a verbal jig!

People and Things

In America preceding the Second World War, to make do with as little as possible as long as possible was pressing need and popular passion. Since the Second World War America's growing appetite for ever new material things has been increasingly more whetted by the world of advertisement. From anxious conservers we have become compulsive consumers.

Are we the better for this transition?
Has the environment benefited?
Serious reflection is long overdue!

In Purgatory or Limbo

*B*ereft of our comforting verities, we are adrift in a sea of uncertainties, without compass and not knowing whether hell or heaven awaits us. Such is the sorry lot of those whose civilization has slipped into its twilight of decline. With the loss of the thought/behavior rudder and ballast provided by a healthy civilization, the individual is thrown back upon his/her own resources, a colossal challenge to which but few are equal. Chaos will prevail until the seeds of a new civilization sprout and spread. May that not be too long in the coming!

Deadly Extremes

*T*he feisty, aggressive and berserk extremes of West and East are on center stage and are determined to battle it out. Madness prevails, nothing is off limits and the booty is political and economic power. Both camps are cut from the same cloth! These testosterone-driven extremes are having their day. Let's hope that each will soon exhaust the other and that both will soon go away.

A pox on all such madmen!

Hope and Folly, Hand in Hand

*F*or many American men, Eastern European women seem to have become more attractive and desirable than local American belles. And for many Eastern European women, American men have become more financially attractive than their local yokels. A coincidence with promise for more than just the lovelorn! Where opportunity beckons, entrepreneurs are ever ready to accommodate—for a price, of course. Agencies on both sides of the Atlantic have quickly sprung up to facilitate the love encounter of America and Europe. Meetings abroad and

meetings at home have been followed by marriage and happiness, but also, and more often by marriage, disillusionment and divorce. Unwarranted hope and questionable adventure!
But then, nothing ventured, nothing gained!

The American Family

Life in America was once a family continuum of blood, place, religion and tradition. A meaningful cohesive whole! Today, American life is largely a continuum of nomadic individuals little conscious of lineage, indifferent to belief and oblivious of the past. A whole has lost its wholeness!

Things Come and Things Go

Like the Industrial Revolution before it, our Electronics Age began as an awesome boon, and
Like the Industrial Revolution, the Electronics Age will in due time end as an irksome bane.
Nothing is good but that it is also bad,
And nothing is here to stay!

The Dark Side of Life

Humans are more fascinated by and preoccupied with the dark than the light side of life, more taken with sickness, sin, evil, crime, deviation, lie, alcoholism, prostitution, masochism, sadism etc. than with their positive counterpossibilities. Our legal system is predominantly preoccupied with life's dark side, as too is our medical world, the world of entertainment even more so, and the news media is totally given to it. The meager attractions of the light side of life seem always to have paled before the general allure of life's more seductive dark side.

American Television

*W*hat is it but fragmented flighty imagery laced with jarring musical sound effects and agitated by a nervous play of light. Words have yielded to enticing impressions that serve the hungry business world. All has become little more than sedative and seduction for the mind, candy and appetizer for the eye, and a restless blur of product, sex and violence for the memory.

Dreams

*T*he myth of America would have us believe that little is beyond the reach of the individual socially and economically, and that the individual need only be prepared to expend the necessary time and energy to realize hopes and dreams. This is certainly true of the few. The many fall exhausted, confused and disenchanted by the wayside! Notwithstanding, the myth lives on and continues to motivate. It is to the resultant passion and energy that America owes its economic hegemony, its dominance in the sciences and its imperialistic world might. The power of dreams should never be underestimated!

Nota Bene

*A*void sentences that consciously congratulate themselves, that are obviously more show than substance and that are little more than verbal acting and not action. Display is the life blood of the world of advertisement, the death of good writing!

People possessed by ideology are the deadliest friends of mankind. Blinders of whatever ilk dehumanize!

All-consuming consumerism has become America's latest passion. Anything to dull any awareness of our existential boredom or agony! Some read to grow,

More, to fortify their views,
Most, to be entertained,
Few, for edification.
Paranoia, bigotry and chauvinism together with radical individualism and unfettered capitalism spell America of the 21stcentury. Our founding fathers, in political heaven looking down at their United States of America, are surely maintaining that this was not their dream!

A Critical Choice

Most people have always been educated or trained in keeping with the needs and interests of society. Traditionally, the few were educated and the many trained. In America, it was not until the 20th century that education overtook and then left training in its wake. Unfortunately, this shift of function to person was of short duration. The wellbeing of the 21st century of electronics and technology clearly depends more upon the trained than upon the educated. The young will again become means and not end, and as always, in the name of progress. This makes for a good living but not a rich life!

Polar Approaches

There is confrontation and that spells fight and victory for the stronger! There is discussion and that implies reflective exchange and victory for the more persuasive!
The former is the more ready and the easier tactic but also the decidedly more futile!
The latter is the more challenging and demanding tactic but also the more promising!
The U.S.A. has almost always opted for action rather than for words. Iraq was but our latest mischoice.

The Rich and the Poor

The gap between the wealthy and the poor in the U.S.A. is appalling, and the gap between the world's wealthy and poor nations is no less distressing. These circumstances can only spawn envy, discontent and hostility. More humanity, good will and generosity would do wonders. A change for the better, unfortunately, is not yet visible on the horizon!

The Now and the Me

America is a "now" society and that "now" is rapidly spreading throughout the world. Yesterday is a "was" and tomorrow a matter of no more concern. In America the "now" is coupled with the "me" and this, too, is gradually spreading throughout the world. All this hardly augurs a better world of tomorrow. But then, tomorrow is of little concern! That is, until it becomes today and affects "me."

Business

In business there has been a subtle and profitable shift of focus from the strength of the product to the weakness of the consumer. Business has made a profitable tool of psychology!

Jewish Immigrants

Humor, music, acumen and persistence guaranteed success for the some 3 million Jews who streamed into America from the eighties of the 19th century to the twenties of the 20th century. Theirs was a success unprecedented, a success that left a positive imprint upon America that has remained indelible.

Time and Space

Time is determined by the speed of light (Einstein).
Time equals space and space, time (Einstein).
Time is the space between changes in things and happenings (Mileck).

Cultural Acceleration

The coming and going of world-changing revolutions has accelerated dangerously. The agricultural revolution dragged on for some 3000 years, the industrial revolution ran its course in some 300 years, and the electronics revolution is likely to exhaust itself in a hundred years. An exciting and dangerous acceleration! Human adaptation has its time demands. Too little time to adapt will leave too many people intellectually confused and emotionally unsettled, and this means a spontaneously combustible culture.

Hypocrisy

"America is a nation founded on the principle that all human life is sacred." This has become Bush's fervent mantra, but only when it serves his purposes. His condoning of assassinations and ready recourse to war appear to be exempt from this very laudable and often repeated principle. Hypocrisy in the White house is alive and in good health!

Love

Love, whether erotic or platonic, like all other instinctive appetites, eludes reason and choice, knows no lasting satisfaction, is dulled by excess, rejuvenated by change, and dies with age. One is not master of but mastered by this compelling drive.

Essayistic Ventures and Topical Asides

The Family Today

*R*adical individualism, work, consumerism and financial pressures have shriveled private family life to an alarming degree. Husband and wife have become progressively more self-centered, ever more consumed by their jobs, leisurely family time has become a thing of the past, and too many children are being left too early to their own devices. What does this hold in store for society at large? Only time will tell!

Truth

*M*ankind's victories are always provisional. This is no less true of scientific than of religious or philosophical truths. Truth like being is a constant becoming. Nor is this spot of wisdom an exception.

The Other

*R*egardless of country of birth, the different peoples of our planet are all human beings, and physically we are all but variations on a theme. However, physical similarity is where our similarity by and large ends. From country to country and particularly from culture to culture people are decidedly different: different in religious, philosophical and political thought, in aspirations, expectations, sensibilities, loves and hates and consequent styles of life and dress. From culture to culture, we are foreigners, strangers, the other, the unknown, the troubling and feared and ultimately hated. And all this too often ends in strife and bloody war. Furthermore, nothing will change until we begin earnestly to try to understand, appreciate, indeed respect and not continue to suspect or try to refashion the different other.

Homo Americanus

The typical American has become so preoccupied making money and spending it, and so possessed by the trivia of television, that no time or interest is left for serious thought. He has become a patsy for the politician.

Outsourcing

After the 18th century humans grew tired of taxing their bodies, and after the 20th century they became tired of trying their brains.

We have been liberated to a remarkable degree from physical toil by machines, tools and appliances, and both to physical benefit and physical detriment.

And computer technology has relieved us of many of our onerous mental labors, and again to mental advantage and disadvantage.

In both instances profit is immediate and obvious. Relief! And in both cases price is exacted slowly and imperceptibly. Our bodies have become flabby and our minds are being automatized!

This individual outsourcing of the physical and the mental anticipated our national outsourcing of industrial and business brawn and brains. The latter is proving to be no less double-edged than the former!

Brawn and Brains

Industrial brawn and ambition were America's making,
Military brawn and bravado are likely to be its unmaking.
Brawn has almost spent itself.
Brains and humanity have yet to assert themselves!
Will they do so before it is too late?
This remains to be seen.
Time is running out!

Tenacity

*T*hanks largely to wits and not to brawn, Jews have managed ably to deflect the slings and arrows of an anti-Semitism that has persisted for some 2000 years.

Thanks largely to brawn and not to wits, American blacks have managed to survive their slavery of some 300 years.

Realities

*C*hange and time are inseparably linked. No change, no measurable time! Change is primary and change is predicated upon a reality, a thing. But for things, there is no space, no measurable space. Things are ultimately primary, our primary realities. Change is a secondary reality, and its results, space and time, are tertiary realities. Like things, consciousness—thoughts and emotions—is a primary reality. Here again change brings with it space and time.

Surges

*O*urs is a decade of surges. For the stock market, surges are old hat. What rises will fall and what falls will rise again! On the other hand, Bush's educational surge at home and his military surge in Iraq are quite novel and troublingly alike. Bush's "we will not leave Iraq without victory" is a military equivalent of his educational "no child will be left behind" banner. Both surges were strongly opposed by a majority of Americans, both are faltering despite their stubborn official pursuit, there is no light at the end of the tunnel for either, and in both cases, failure will in due time be stamped "mission accomplished."

The "decider" Bush will have his way and America will be left to pay! Unwarranted and ill-advised political surges!

Idle Grumblings

*M*ost of our appliances are too complicated to be repaired.

Most of our contracts are too obscure to be understood.

Most legal language is beyond lay comprehension.

Most packages are too tightly sealed for ready opening.

Content specifics of most packaged food are too scientifically specific to be helpful.

The text of footnote disclaimers is characteristically too long to invite reading and/or the print is too small for ready reading.

Use directions are all too often either too telegrammic or too detailed to be useful to the average person.

Too much of today's literary scholarship—isoteric trivia wrapped in obscure jargon—is quite unintelligible, and not only to the layman.

George Bush's America is plaintiff, jury and judge, and so was Hitler's Germany, Mussolini's Italy and Stalin's Russia, and for each of these messianic leaders, war was a crusade to secure the homeland and to better the world.

Globalization

*A*merica's globalizing of capitalism is nothing more than a globalization of aggressive selfishness!

America's efforts to globalize American democracy are an exercise in futility!

America's professed mission to globalize American freedom is little more than political ploy!

Our Surveyors and Purveyors

*W*e must have historians to keep alive the facts of the past.

We must have thinkers to preoccupy themselves with and to add to the best thought of the past.

But for such surveyors and purveyors a culture's account would be but a lean short story and not the grand novel it is.

People

The diehard pessimist glowers in the shadow of his gloom, the inveterate optimist radiates in the glow of his exuberance and most of the many between these extremes just shuffle along slightly baffled, hoping for the best and unprepared for the worst.

Definitions: A Bit of Metaphysics

Direct definition of reality eludes mind and language. Reality—abstract, concrete, actional—is defined by description, composition, association and function, or self-referentially (a stone is a stone, love is love, to run is to run). Attributive and referential explanation are the extent of possible definition! Referential explanation is circular, and attributes are themselves realities that defy definitions no less than the realities they qualify. It appears that realities are simply beyond human ken.

In today's definitional confrontation with reality, we deal with attributes.
In his plumbing of reality, Plato dealt with shadows in a cave.
In metaphysics, progress progresses mighty slowly!

Music

What is music but sound that is the panacea of panaceas, the opiate of opiates, the analgesic of analgesics, the attraction of attractions, the stimulant of stimulants, the obsession of obsessions, the purgative of purgatives, the aphrodisiac of aphrodisiacs, the gift of gifts, the food of foods, our timeless and universal elixir!

Cultural Twilight

A culture gradually wilts and eventually dies when its core body of religious beliefs together with its satellite body of morality and values does not change in a manner commensurate with the changing times. No accommodating changes mark the pending demise of a culture, drastic changes the possible birth of a new culture. Our Western culture has outgrown its aging rigid Judeo/Christian core, but continues to pay lip service to it, but only for want of any emerging new body of beliefs and values. Until that time, our chaotic culture will continue its rudderless course!

For the Absolute and the Relative

*T*he language of beliefs, truths and values that was inherited by the age of relativity, ushered in by Einstein, was a language that in meaning was attuned to the world of absolutes that had preceded Einstein. That same language, with but a shift from absolute meaning to relative meaning, now serves our age of relativity as well as the age of absolutes had been served by its language. What once had been absolutely the case—this is right, wrong, good, bad, true, false, etc.—is now only relatively so! Pre-relativists understand one another perfectly well, as do post-absolutists. A class of misunderstanding and animosity inevitably ensues when "Pres" and "Posts" intermingle in serious argument.

Literary Pundits

*S*ince the last quarter of the last century, too many literary scholars, critics, and theorists have become constipated gasbags. In their wake, they have left a paucity of insight, let alone wisdom, and a plentitude of intellectual farts that do little more than excite the olfactory nerve. Some wags would argue that this has always been the case.

Change

*T*he Western World has become passionately enamored of electronics,
Even its teachers value the computer more than the humanities.
Matter is rapidly yielding to means,
Humans to robots and culture to technocracy!
Not all change is change for the better!

A Trend

*I*n our troubled modern Western World, a once disturbing individual inclination has rapidly become a very startling widespread trend. Disenchanted young idealists, once starry-eyed dreamers, are rapidly becoming troubled skeptics, who quickly morph into resigned agnostics, who, in turn, soon end as mild then bitter cynics. Is this the beginning of an end and the start of a new beginning?

The Wealthy and the Poor

*L*ittle affection is lost between America's wealthy and its poor.
Disdain and indifference, more than commiseration, characterizes the attitude of the haves to the have-nots.
Envy and suspicion, more than admiration, characterizes the attitude of the have-nots to the haves.
Both camps could do with a little more knowledge of the other, and with a good dose of brotherly love.
The other can become a brother!

What is Life?

*F*or some life is but a series of chance happenings and consequent chance feelings and chance thoughts.

For others, all happenings and the feelings and thoughts elicited are cause and effect accountable. For still others all is fate determined. And many others ascribe all to the will of God.

Then there are those, perhaps the majority, who are moved by but not committed to any one of these beliefs and who have selective recourse to all four to account for life and its imponderables.

Chacun à son goût, as the French would have it!

The Spirit and the Flesh

For many, who are given to the Christian belief in the purity of the spirit and in the questionableness of the flesh, the sodomy of homosexuality is sinful and disgusting, and the congress of heterosexuality is only slightly less tainted and distasteful. These folks, like most devout souls, are troubled by what is and enamored with what should be!

The Actual and the Spiritual

Mankind has never been content just to wallow thoughtlessly in reality's mucky mess. Human beings have always sought explanations for, and relief from their wanting selves and their wanting world. They have always found explanation and relief in the notion of a better, a spiritual self, and a better, a spiritual world. This belief in a spiritual realm beyond the physical world has always, in due time, become a religion providing expected elucidation and solace. Religion, in turn and in time, and thanks to belief's eventual and inevitable paling and demise, has always become a dated social institution, leaving mankind at a loss again, and again anxious to seek explanation and relief in a new belief. New belief has always been but a variant of old belief and the former's lot has always been but a repetition of the latter's. This cycle is likely to continue just as long as mankind and the world remain essentially what they have always been!

Essayistic Ventures and Topical Asides

Absurdity

On the fifth anniversary of the Iraq war, President Bush, proudly and with his usual smirk, summed up its benefits: "The world is better and the United States of America is safer."

Tell that to the 4000 American soldiers killed and to the 40,000 wounded; to the hundreds of thousands of Iraqis killed and injured and to the millions of refugees; to the citizens of a country laid waste, and to the citizens of a country that has foolishly squandered hundreds of billions of borrowed dollars.

Absurdity knows no moderation!

Universities

Universities, once institutions of learning run by culture-minded academics and intent primarily upon a liberal arts education, have become money-minded corporations governed by non-academic administrations and highly-paid CEOs, and focussed primarily upon professionalism. Adventure has become investment!

Technology

The electronic age of technology is primarily concerned about and pre-occupied with means and ends, with little interest in substance. To those given to this burgeoning fascination, the traditional world of thought holds little attraction and the traditional imponderables, none at all.

Illusions

There are those who believe that science and technology have all the answers to all of our problems. What naïve souls! Their days of belief are just as numbered as were those of the religiously, philosophically and culturally inclined idealists preceding them.

A Success Story

*W*hile nations have always featured their victories, the Jewish people has always celebrated its endless defeats—among them, slavery in Egypt, Babylonian exile, destruction of its temple by the Romans, the Diaspora and anti-Semitism, the Holocaust. Defeats did not break the Jews, they only made them more stubborn and gave them the strength necessary to continue to cling to their Jewishness and to their Jewish tradition. The Jews made success of defeat, have survived in spite of, and today flourish! Theirs is an enviable example of human resilience, adaptability, determination, tenacity and ingenuity and of human possibility. An amazing success story!

In Search of Answers

*H*umans, with the beginning of their ability to think, embarked upon a mental odyssey motivated by questions about life and the world at large. This adventure of the mind has left a myriad of tentative but no final truths in its wake. Questions have found their transitory answers and answers have only posed new questions to be answered. Final answers, absolute truths have and will always be beyond human grasp. Though intrinsically futile, mankind's odyssey of the mind has been a magnificent, exciting and highly rewarding venture. But for their intellectual curiosity, humans would still be cavorting in the tree tops!

George Washington

*I*n his farewell speech to his fellow countrymen, a prescient George Washington warned against both political and commercial imperialism. This warning, by and large, fell on deaf ears and America is the worse for it.

Truths

*T*here is no absolute up or down, in or out, right or wrong, good or bad, cheap or expensive, tall or short, bright or stupid, wet or dry, joyful or sad, soft or hard et cetera.
Whatever is, is only in terms of relationship.
Truth is not something absolute but only that which is deemed to be true.
We live by relative truths, our cultural truths.

Intents

Christianity is intent upon a perfection of the self,
Buddhism upon the extinction of the self,
Confucianism opts for a better social self and
Taoism for the tranquil self.

Beyond the Pale

*A*merica has long had a love affair with the outsider, the outlaw, loner, rogue, gangster, trespasser, dissenter, with the maverick who chooses to go his own unconventional way and to do his own unconventional thing, as epitomized in Frank Sinatra's "I did it my way." Indeed, America itself has become and has perhaps always been a maverick nation. And this is but a national expression of America's radical individualism, which, in turn, is but our early-day frontiersmanship in modern garb.

Holy Wars

*P*resident Bush insists that America has a "Messianic Mission to spread Democracy throughout the world." Vice-President candidate Sarah Palin maintains that America's "troops are on a task from God."

We are back to the Holy Wars of yore!
We surely have come a long way, baby!

Our Thoughts

*M*ost of everyman's daily thinking consists of a stream of unfinished fleeting thoughts. Except when we are in deep sleep or in a comatose state, our brains are ever active. We lead exceedingly busy lives and our rapidly shifting flow of thoughts reflects this. But, except for the thinking writers among us, we rarely have time to, or care to let even a few of our thoughts evolve and conclude. Instead, we traffic by and large in conventional thought, nipping our own in the bud. We all have ideas, notions, persuasions, that is to say our truths, but most of these are the common coin to which we have come by more or less by accident and not by effort. The Western world might do well to adopt a more leisurely life style. Less time necessary for earning a livelihood and more time to do with as one pleases could make for much less conventional and appreciably more original thought. And this could lead to an abode better suited for human beings than our present manic world.

The Bubble

*O*ur present international financial market crisis is clearly primarily of and in the developed world. A fragile financial system was destined to collapse. Exuberantly avaricious private enterprise left largely to regulate itself knew no limits. The bubble grew and the bubble burst, as all bubbles do.

America's bubble was the largest and Americans will have to pay the highest price.

A painfully expensive lesson in economics!

Will we learn?

Life

*L*ife in all of its countless forms is but a tenacious force, a relentless drive, a blind passion intent exclusively upon self-preservation and self-perpetuation. Evolution was born of this all-thrust and culture of this inevitable evolution.

Did life begin with the alleged "big bang?"

If so—why?

And why the "big bang?"

It always begins with questions, is always followed by new answers and always ends in new whys!

A Cause for Pause

*I*n America, a competent college football coach is clearly more highly valued than a competent college professor.

Per annum, the former can expect two to three million dollars and the latter from 100 to 125 thousand dollars.

Surely a cause for pause!

Science and Religion

*S*cience and religion are brother-sister worlds.

Religion is a comforting quest, a spiritual adventure, and an intoxicating binge of imagination.

Science is an explanative quest, a cerebral adventure and a binge of thought.

What is belief but pious hope!

What is science but tentative conviction!

Religion is belief,

Science is fact,

And truth may be a blend of both!

Joseph Mileck

The Gain and Bane of Technology

*T*oday's technology has obviously afforded almost everybody bounteous benefits and comforts. That we have been and are paying a considerable price for technology's life-enhancing "things"—indeed, that
we have become something of a victim of technology—is less obvious,
though no less a fact. We created technology and technology, in turn,
has refashioned us, has changed our thinking and the scope and
focus of our thought, has conditioned our feelings, altered our values,
directed our interests and revolutionized the way we work, play and
live. In this sweeping change, the focus of attention has clearly shifted
from the human being to "things." Technology's converts would argue
that all has changed for the better. Humanists would contend that the
price for technology's blessings has been too high.

Time will tell!

Outsourcing

*W*hatever can be automated or routinized will sooner or later be
outsourced for cheaper production. The Western World is shifting
from industrial plant to front office, and the Third World countries
are moving from farm to industrial plant.

A windfall for America's wily capitalists,

A godsend for the hungry masses abroad,

A poison pill for America's industrial workers!

Newspapers and Books

*T*he Electronics Age appears to be making the demise of our traditional newspapers and books inevitable. In addition to much else,
newspapers have been our watch dogs. For these watch dogs to leave
the scene would be an irreparable loss for society. Internet newspapers

in the hands of amateur reporters are a poor substitute for our handy, professionally-run daily papers.

Books, too, are likely to go the unfortunate way of our newspapers, and for the same financial reason. Like Internet newspapers, Internet books—avoid as they do the traditional peer review and the publication costs—are less costly, but they are also decidedly less authoritative. And like Internet newspapers, Internet books are also decidedly less comfortable in their use than their traditional counterparts. In both cases, too much is lost for too little reason!

International Relations

*P*resident Barack Obama seems intent upon inaugurating a new phase in American diplomacy. America's exceptionalism and unilateralism of the past half century managed to foster more international anger and rancor than admiration and friendship. America, the alleged birthplace of modern democracy, clearly did not become the enviable exemplary nation that President G.W. Bush imagined it to be. President Obama appears to be determined to replace Bush's imperialistic arrogance, his suspicion and threat, with more understanding, mutual respect and meaningful dialogue. A drastic change in American diplomacy! Negotiations with such as Cuba, Iran, Korea and the Muslim world at large, without America's usual categorical pre-conditions and self-serving reservations, would be an auspicious beginning for President Obama's new American diplomacy. We shall in due time see if America the supernation is willing to become a nation among nations.

An Economic Dilemma

*E*conomists of stature would have Americans believe that America's economic recovery depends upon ample credit and more borrowing and spending—the very cause of America's boom and bust. Americans are urged to borrow and to spend and at the same time to save, for without savings, America's economic well-being would be jeopardized. To preclude a chronic pendulation from financial mania to financial depression, discreet spending and discreet saving have become imperative. This delicate balancing of opposites could put an end to adventurous financial surges and disastrous recessions and would probably also close the horrendous gap between America's extremely wealthy few and its many less fortunate few.

Space and Time

The modern world is possessed by a two-pronged passion: the virtual elimination of space and time. Ever more rapid transportation, ever more rapid production and ever more rapid communication are the order of the day. Everything is becoming ever more intensified in its steady shrinkage. Mankind's physical, mental and psychological fibers are being ever more sorely taxed. When will they reach their limits of stress and what will be the consequences?

The Information Revolution

The human brain has its limits no less than the human body. An endless flood of unfiltered information is likely to lay waste a person no less than a tsunami leaves a landscape in tatters. How much can the mind accommodate and how much can it process? Does the mind have a safety valve to stem the flow of invading information? Will the mind's ability to process an ever-increasing flow of information grow proportionally with the growing stream of information? Will the information revolution spawned by the electronics age eventually overburden and incapacitate the human mind, or will the brain evolve to meet the challenge, or will humans simply learn to absorb and to digest information ever more economically and selectively?
Time will tell!

Humanism

*I*t is high time that the world's best minds shift their attention from the profitable novelties of the Electronics Age to a more deserving challenge: the human being. Society would undoubtedly be the better for a renaissance in psychology and psychiatry.

Freud, Jung and their pioneer confreres have been kept waiting too long for a new breakthrough in their field.

Pills are not enough. Startling new insights are necessary!

Either/Or

*H*omogeneity facilitates.

Heterogeneity challenges.

France's homogeneity persuaded Montesquieu to argue that successful self-government depends upon the commonality of homogeneity. America's heterogeneity persuaded its founding fathers to insist that successful democracy depends upon the creative contentiousness of heterogeneity.

Montesquieu's was a positive embrace of the reality that was France. America's founding fathers' was no less a positive embrace of the reality that was the United States.

Both contentions regarding good government had merit in the 18th century. They still have merit today but only with a reminder that good government is ultimately impossible without a citizenry that is duly informed, thoughtful and humane.

Differences of Opinion

*T*here will always be differences of opinion in both matters significant and matters of little import. Courteous dialogue can resolve many of these differences, but most firmly entrenched disagreements are irreconcilable. When the latter is the case, when civil argument has been of no avail, opponents should simply agree to disagree and then go their separate ways

Watch your Tongue

*T*hanks to the electronics world of today, the English language is being commonly tormented as never before. Apart from its telegrammic distortion of syntax and its excess of contrived abbreviations, short-lived slang and quirky neologisms, our commonly-written and commonly-spoken English of today has become pockmarked by words and phrases misused or used too frequently and for no good reason.

Many adverbs—e.g., literally, actually, truly, basically, frankly, obviously, absolutely, exactly, simply—have become indispensable ornamentation, and too many interjections—e.g., you know, you know what I mean, you know what I'm saying, I mean, the fact of the matter is, if you would, or whatever—have become annoying gratuitous ejecta. Our English has become burdened by superfluous irksome verbal stuffing. Better a brief pause for thought than annoying dog-eared filler!

The Final Chapter

*A*merica's growing number of assisted-living/nursing homes are institutions no less depressing than its many somber funeral parlours. The former warehouse the infirm and dying elderly and the later dispose of the dead. A doleful institutionalized finale!

The close and end of life might better be in familiar surroundings and with family and friends. Such would be more personal, more comforting and more humane, and not something to be dreaded.

Justice?

America's military tribunals for alleged enemy combatants and terrorists are kangaroo courts!

The judges are appointed by the Pentagon.

The jury is selected by military commanders.

The military may monitor defense lawyer's conversations with their clients.

Confessions made under physical or mental pressure are admissible.

There is no ban on evidence from illegal searches.

Defendants can be convicted on the basis of hearsay of someone whom the defense never gets to see or question.

And but for the death sentence, jurors can convict by a non-unanimous vote.

America's highly-touted justice for all appears to have become rather selective!

America's Free-wheeling Capitalism

America's financial institutions—free market capitalism interested primarily in maximizing profits and persuaded that rules are only for fools—precipitated America's financial débacle.

This casino financial world shelved fiscal restraint, left Washington with a chronic budget deficit, made light of a swelling trade deficit, tolerated an ever-growing appalling national debt, and financed the world's most expensive military and the world's largest mass of nuclear weapons.

Free-wheeling market economy has had its dismal day. It may be high time America turn to a more regulated social market economy.

A Questionable Modus Operandi

Countries that do not enjoy America's stamp of approval are arbitrarily relegated to its list of enemy countries, and all enemy countries, by definition, pose a threat to America's security. Such countries must obviously be addressed imperatively and checkmated forcibly.

This has long been America's prevailing conviction and customary *modus operandi!*

Management and Labor

*I*f America's national economy is to remain sound and is to continue to be a leading world economy, its industry/business complex and their unions have to put an end to their adversary relationship. The longtime battle between management and labor was inevitable and probably necessary to establish a working relationship acceptably mindful of the needs and aspirations of both camps. But times have changed and unless the present management-labor relationship changes for the better, America's national economy is likely soon to be in jeopardy. Adversaries have to become associates, have to become a team intent upon producing the best at the lowest cost in order to be able to compete with the world's expanding industries.

Expediency and Morality

*M*orality but rarely trumps expediency!

The Noble Lie for the common good was defended by Plato in his *Republic*, became the hallmark of all despotic régimes, and was the moral imperative of President G.W. Bush's White House. Here expediency paraded brazenly in moral garb. Was America and is America exceptional in this regard? Hardly! Expediency and not morality has always and everywhere been the order of the day.

Expediency is mankind's preferred existential recourse.

Christianity

*C*hristianity's supernatural narrative long fascinated the Western world, offered persuasive answers for life's imponderables, provided just moral direction and afforded needed comfort and solace. Such is no longer the case. With the passing of centuries, attractive myth slowly but surely became antiquated belief. All things have their day, then fade away, yielding to a new fascination. Such is life!

Globalization

*T*he world is experiencing a gradual global levelling off:
English has become our global mode of communication;
Science has become global;
The business world is rapidly becoming global;
Music and the arts know no political boundaries;
National literatures are becoming ever more international;
Professional sports are pursued internationally;
Foods have spread far beyond their national boundaries;
Travel has linked the farthest reaches of the globe;
And ethnically and racially mixed marriages are on the rise.
If this global trend persists, our national states and diverse religions may well, in due time, also coalesce.
There is some promise of a hopefully better world to come.
But it will take some time, and luck!

Memorable Words

*P*residential addresses are characteristically more ceremony than substance, or more political than profound, or more sweetness than light. Occasionally, however, a pithy sentence, very reflective of both the speaker and the times, stands out and lives on. This has happened three times since our 32nd president.

President Franklin Delano Roosevelt (1933–1945) will forever be remembered for his "we have nothing to fear but fear itself."

President John Fitzgerald Kennedy (1961–1963) roused a healthy patriotism with his "ask not what the country can do for you but what you can do for your country."

President Barack Hussein Obama's (2008–2016) inaugural "a nation cannot prosper long when it favors only the prosperous" was a foretelling shot across the bow.

Nero Fiddled While Rome Burned

*I*n the midst of international tumult and critical domestic problems, while the world was figuratively burning and our country was in national turmoil, Middle America was taken with Britney Spear's pantless buttocks, with Simpson the Juice and his nefarious activities and with Michael Jackson's ignominious demise.

What does this tell us about Mr. And Mrs. America?!

A Change is in Order

*A*merica needs ever more new technology to produce ever more ever more rapidly. The health of its economy and contentment of its people depends upon this steady acceleration.

This gives cause for pause!

Perhaps America's radical individualism and consumerism and unfettered capitalism are in need of some modification.

Our Things

*I*n our electronics age, we are scurrying so rapidly from good to better, to yet better products, that we no longer have time to understand or to develop an intimate relationship with our *things*.

This may be more loss than gain!

America's Psyche on Display

*M*yspace, Facebook, Twitter *et alia* are seismographs that reveal America's psychology. The country's language and mood, its thoughts and feelings, wants and needs, hopes and fears, loves and hates and its activities and aspirations are all fully exposed to every curious ear and eye. Americans have chosen a public podium to air themselves. It will surely not be long before America's psychoanalytical institutions have much to proclaim.

The Science of Human Relationships

*W*hile the hard sciences have been pursued with a passion in the past half century, the study of psychology has been just lumbering along. Except medically, human beings have been given short shrift. We know more and more about things and, relatively speaking, less and less about people. Human relationships have always been complex and challenging; they have become fraught with anxieties, hostilities, fears and hatred in America's ethnically-fragmented society of today. A renaissance in psychology is overdue. The Science of Human Relationships is a pursuit whose time has come! When individual relationships improve, it will only be a matter of time before international relationships follow suit.

Hallucinations Galore

America has been hallucinating for quite some time. It sees *fires* when there are none. It spent years fighting a *fire* in Vietnam, has for years been fighting *fires* in Afghanistan and Iraq, and is now trying desperately to convince the world at large that *fires* are about to break out in North Korea and in Iran. Delusional America is also convinced, and is trying to convince all nations willing to lend an ear, that all of these imagined and potential *fires* are a serious threat not only to America's security but also to the very security of the world.

Freedom

Freedom for the sake of freedom is as sterile and as circumscribed as art for art's sake, love for love's sake, wealth for wealth's sake, punishment for punishment's sake, etc. Meaningfulness is found in context and not in a vacuum. To become personally and socially meaningful, freedom for the sake of freedom must become freedom from what and for what.

Unqualified Freedom

Unqualified freedom is a figment of the imagination. Each person is bound by personal needs, wants and expectations, and by life's demands and social circumstances. At best, we are more bound than free and the more complete and richer for it.

In America, we have made a veritable fetish of our unqualified freedom. Anything that allegedly curtails our freedom is reflexively suspect and summarily dismissed by Mr. and Mrs. America. Nationalized healthcare systems, common in industrialized nations of the world, have become anathema in America. The advocates of private enterprise—in this case, the pharmaceutical industry and insurance corporations—had only to inform the general public that any national healthcare system is a serious threat to individual freedom. No more than a serial repetition of this blatant lie has been necessary to cast a pall over any and every form of government-run medical care.

Nuclear Weapons

A resolve by the clique of nations that harbors arsenals of nuclear weapons to bar any further nuclear tests and to prevent any further proliferation of nuclear weapons, is both highly laudable and seriously suspect. Not to believe that these nuclear powers that be clearly have a hidden vested interest in such a ban and curtailment, is to be politically naïve. What better tactic for these nations to preserve the power of their nuclear clout? A nefarious intent in the guise of virtue!

Strife

The world is rife with strife: economic, political and military. Friction and hostility characterize the human community, and this has always been the case.

It is quite clear that man does not live by bread alone.

Violence nurtures his soul.

The Catholic Church would call this original sin!

The medical world might call it essential proclivity!

Mysteries

The mysterious, the secret, the unknown and the perplexing have always been more fascinating and disturbing than the transparent and rationally graspable, just as the claire-obscure of twilight has always been more intriguing than the revealing glare of midday. Mysteries are the shadows that invite flights of the imagination that take us far beyond pedestrian realities and mystery unraveled returns us to commonplace earth.

The more romantic human beings, those given more to the imagination than to reason, treasure and nurture their mysteries and enjoy a perpetual orgy of possibilities. The more rational, the more matter-of-fact among us, like the Greek Archimedes, shout *heurēka* when they unknot their mysteries.

The world and life are replete with and will remain replete with mysteries. Romantic dreamers will forever feed on these mysteries and sober scientists will forever provide their explanations.

C'est la vie!

Guise and Actuality

*A*merica's sporadic Indian Wars from 1775 to 1895 were primarily intent upon land expansion and country building. America's present-day recurrent military interaction with smaller countries far beyond its borders has been primarily motivated by its dreams of a modern empire.

Variations on a theme! *Plus ça change, plus c'est la même chose.*

In its alleged determination to civilize and to christianize its native Indians, America was prepared, if necessary, to exterminate them. In its alleged determination to democratize and to deed with freedom a number of smaller backward nations, America has been prepared since 1950 to beat them to a pulp. Both enterprises were folly and error. Both laudably guised but decidedly less laudably motivated ventures left a bloody trail in their wake.

Subterfuge has always been a reliable ruse!

Health Care

America's medical care is badly in need of change. Serious change is unlikely even though the majority of Americans are in favor of, are indeed almost demanding real change, and even though the necessary financing is not beyond reach.

Politics is the problem. Republicans and Democrats are too preoccupied checkmating each other to focus on national concerns, and the army of lobbyists in Washington is stoking the fray.

Power and money are the flies in the ointment!

A Pre- not Post-Achievement Award

On the 9th of October, the Nobel Prize Committee announced that President Obama was the recipient of the Nobel Peace Prize for 2009. Oslo's choice raised eyebrows and was dismissed by many as something of a joke. That the president of a country at war simultaneously in Iraq and Afghanistan and severely at odds with North Korea and Iran should be honored for furthering world peace was understandably for many a perplexing travesty. But the award was neither joke nor travesty but astute psychological politics.

President Obama was awarded the Nobel Peace Prize clearly less for peace-furthering achievement than in a hopeful anticipation of an eventual contribution to world peace. Obama's feet were put to the fire. Should President Obama rise to this challenge and manage to begin America's hoped-for conversion from a country of war to a country of peace, the prize committee's studied gamble will have been more than amply rewarded. Time will tell!

Cultural Decline

Distrust of politicians throughout the Western World has become commonplace, and for good reason. Politicians have by and large become a bunch of corrupt, dishonest and opportunistic megalomaniacs. Indeed, many of their shenanigans verge upon criminality. Such is inevitable when individual inhibition and traditional social prohibitions cease to persuade or to compel.

What is taking place in the political world is but one of the more obvious of the many prevailing social symptoms marking the decline of the Western Judeo-Christian culture.

We are in for a rough ride before the dawn of a new cultural era!

Governments and Their People

There is almost always a distressing discrepancy between what is or is transpiring and what a government chooses to tell its public. This deliberate deception and abuse of trust is the case in America and no less in the rest of the world.

What is divulged is characteristically too rosy or too gloomy. This is known as political expediency, and is always exercised for the general good, or so the powers that be would contend.

A lot less hubris and a lot more trust are in order!

A Persistent Propensity

Today, as commonly in the past, suspicion, hatred and violence characteristically prevail over goodwill, love and peaceful interaction. Some, accounting for this dire propensity theologically, would attribute it to original sin, to the attraction to evil inherent in human beings. Others, preferring to view this propensity biologically, would regard it as but another of the many manifestations of life's never-ceasing reflexive struggle to stay alive. Still others would simply argue wanting enlightenment.

Whatever may be the explanation or explanations, it is high time that this dismal propensity be curbed, and by whatever means.

Idealism Compromised

President Obama's realistic idealism is idealism compromised: idealism politicized, idealism become pragmatic.

Obama's argued righteousness of America's wars in Iraq and Afghanistan is a blend of conceit and delusion of a tragically-conflicted idealist. It is either the high road or the low road. One cannot serve two disparate masters simultaneously.

Wars, good or bad, are means that destroy and kill, and as such, are beyond justification. To argue the contrary is to open Pandora's Box!

Achievers

Achievers are a restless lot, strivers who are never content and doers who never achieve enough and never stop trying to achieve. They are our makers and shakers and they never stop worming and squirming and/or flailing and thrashing.

Achievement is the achiever's way of life!

This can be a blessing or a curse or both.

Parents and Their Children

Parents too often leave their children with too little self-esteem, too little self-confidence and, at worst, with a deep-seated sense of unworthiness. This parental inner imprint determines a child's life to an alarming degree. The child so afflicted is left more often than not struggling frantically to cope with self and life. Psychotherapy can help to blur this deleterious imprint enough to make life tolerable, but it cannot blot it out.

Blessed are those children who have emotionally sound parents, loving and prudent parents who leave them with a healthy store of self-appreciation.

Poets

Serious poets are able to cut through life's tangled mess to get at life's essentials. They are keen observers and students of life. They are a culture's seismograph. They are our Cassandras, our Delphic seers and are to be heeded.

A Return of the Dark Ages

In the world of yesteryear, the voices of the experts carried the day. Then came the Electronics Age and its Internet. Now the cacophony of opinion of the masses is threatening the authority of the informed specialists. Such is today's democracy in action.

Experts are often wrong but the hoi polloi is rarely right!

Continued Exceptionalism

President Obama's recent public assertion in China that America's espoused freedoms are not uniquely American, but that they are universal principles, and as such should be adopted by all other countries, is almost as absurd, though not quite as inflammatory as President Bush's fervent insistence that it is America's messianic mission to spread American democracy throughout the world.

American exceptionalism, though somewhat attenuated, is still alive and well. Modesty continues to be a commodity in short supply.

Idiocracy

The ascent of foolish, witless mediocrities in America's world of politics (e.g. Sarah Palin), the blatantly puerile arguments against any reform in America's medical care by leaders of the Republican Party (e.g. John Boehner) and America's continued pursuit of its futile wars in Iraq and Afghanistan evidence an appalling decline in whatever common sense and prudence America may once have boasted.

America has long been a slopocracy and is now degenerating into an idiocracy.

More thought and less reflex response would better become the world's leading political and economic power.

A Jaundiced View

America is a republic in name alone. It is a kingship in fact. America's presidents are brief pseudo-kings, its financial tycoons are its abiding aristocracy and its people are its obliging commoners. George III of England is probably smirking from his throne in heaven!

Hope and Fear

In America's political world, persuasion by informed rational argument is touted but only rarely practised. Politicians learned long ago that the interest and attention span of Mr. And Mrs. America were limited to the simple slogans that do little more than stir hope and instill fear. Hope of good things to come and fear of bad things in the offing became America's banners of persuasion.

Hope and fear allow politicians to shape both America's domestic and its foreign policy at will and to serve their often-questionable purposes.

Discomfited by informed argument, Mr. and Mrs. America have long fallen all too easy prey to the machinations of their politicians.

Wall Street

The daily shifting numbers posted by the stock market do not reflect the ups and downs of America's economy as much as they are a reflection of the labile emotional state of those who play the market.

Wall Street has become something of a national casino. Its patrons are akin to jittery gamblers.

Reason and Emotions

The emotions are life's non-reflective driving force, its fueled engine. Reason, with recourse to reflection, accommodates or tries to moderate the emotions, that is to say, to control and to steer the engine. More often than not, the reining in of the emotions is anything but successful: the engine rumbles tumultuously and blindly on.

We are primarily emotional creatures and only secondarily creatures of reason. Would that our emotions were less prevailing and would that our reason were more assertive. Life would be less exciting but also decidedly more peaceful!

Religion and Culture

A belief germinates, spreads, becomes a religion and religion, in turn, spawns a culture. Religion and culture wax and peak, then belief wanes and culture fades.

Essayistic Ventures and Topical Asides

Christianity and its culture has reached this twilight stage. Islam and its culture are not far behind.

Spent religions and cultures leave debris in their wake, seeds of belief and thought, some of which eventually sprout and herald a new religion and a new culture.

This evolving course form birth to death is, in variation, reflected in the animal world and no less in the plant world:

A seed germinates, sprouts, grows, flowers, then gradually fades away leaving seeds of renewal behind.

A Clash of Ideologies

The Judeo-Christian world is motivated by a laudable ideology that paradoxically condones assassination and warfare in the name of security.

The Muslim world is motivated by an equally laudable ideology that just as paradoxically condones assassination and warfare in the name of security.

Each camp is convinced that it is right and that the other is wrong and neither camp is about to change its mind.

The future promises little more than prolonged fitful warfare!

A Healthy Democracy

Too many Americans are ignorant by choice, lazy in thought and wanting in goodwill. This has done much to make a slopocracy of our Democracy. A healthy Democracy depends upon the informed, the reflective and the humane.

Government of the People, by the People, for the People.

*W*ere Lincoln alive today, he would be thoroughly disillusioned by the course American government has taken. His hope that America's "government of the people, by the people, for the people shall not perish from this earth" has proved to be but wishful thinking. Government in America has become a raucous political game, "the people" have become little more than pawns and special interests now befuddle the electorate and manipulate Congress in both domestic and foreign matters. To continue to insist that the American government is still of, by and for "the people" is delusional!

Moral Reasoning

*F*or our founding fathers, moral reasoning was to be the very foundation of the American way of life. This *modus operandi* was to remain an espoused ideal until the middle of the 20th century. Since the end of the Second World War and increasingly so with the passing years, the constraints of moral reasoning have become anathema both to America's political and its financial world. These two regal worlds have evolved their own power- and money-minded moralities: all is kosher if it makes for power or ends in profit. America's founding fathers must be having conniptions in their graves!

The Commonweal

*R*epublicans tend to be philosophers. Small government and liberty is their El Dorado.
Democrats tend to be sociologists. Compassion and fairness is their ideal.

Unfortunately, both Republicans and Democrats are also wily politicians—first and foremost—who do not allow their ideological inclinations to curb personal interests. The commonweal is by and large short-changed.

Stimulus Money

*M*oney and opportunity spread best from the financial world down to the public at large: the so-called "downward trickle of prosperity." This was the conviction of President George Bush and this belief persuaded President Obama's Whitehouse to attempt to stimulate America's collapsing economy by financially bolstering most of its largest banks and lending institutions. The hope and belief that these financial powers would resultantly begin quickly to lend more freely and more widely proved to be a pious wish. By way of thanks, the financial world only tightened its credit and even had the gall to invest much of the stimulus money in government securities. So much for the "downward trickle of prosperity" theory!

Left to its own devices, the financial world reflexively saw to itself, little concerned about the growing number of America's unemployed. Had the stimulus money been accompanied by a strict stipulation that credit become immediately and readily available to small businesses, new jobs would fairly quickly have reduced the alarming number of unemployed and America's financial crisis would not have gotten out of hand.

Let's hope that today's hindsight becomes tomorrow's foresight!

America's Trauma

*I*n the past three years, traditional American confidence has been badly shattered, and untraditional American fear has simultaneously spiralled. Americans have been left bewildered by the near collapse of America's mighty financial world and left badly shaken by its questionable and stuttering wars in Iraq and Afghanistan.

Change is clearly in order if future recurrences of the present disarray are to be prevented: The financial world will have to be tightly regulated and America's militant imperialism must become a thing of the past.

If Washington does not rise to the occasion, America's future will be blighted by yet more irrational exuberance and yet more fearful depression.

Time will tell!

Secrecy

That WikiLeaks' exposure of the brazen wheeling and dealing behind the scene in high places is likely to be punished rather than rewarded, is very disturbing. The righteous indignation of the self-absorbed powers that be is pure gall!

"Secrecy for security" seems to have become entrenched in Washington. The right of Americans at large to know what their government is up to both on and off the record, is being unabashedly violated. Official misconduct has found a shield in national security.

This drift of condoned secrecy, if continued and extended surreptitiously, will soon leave America's touted government of, by and for the people in its wake.

Secrecy bodes little good and spawns much mischief!

Undesirable Bubbles

A financial world left free to do what it chose to do, produced a financial bubble that was doomed to burst.

A government left free to do what it chose to do, produced a political-military bubble that is doomed to burst.

Corporate Culture

Corporate culture has become international in its reach, a world unto itself! Its primary goal is maximum profit, it is beholden only to its shareholders, and the social and political consequences of its heavy tread are of incidental concern.

This wayward culture has become to the world of today what aristocracy once was to the Middle Ages. Irresponsible excess doomed feudal aristocracy and socially-blind hubris will hasten the eventual demise of today's corporate culture.

The "Little" of "Much"

The Electronics Age has left both the ordinary many and the exceptional few wallowing in a confusion of information about the somebodies and the nobodies and about things significant and things trivial. Little is redacted and even less digested and most quickly becomes a blur.

This plethora of ephemera has become standard entertainment, a never-ending soap opera, fast-moving distraction and not food for thought. And what is revelled in today is forgotten by tomorrow. *Too much* has paradoxically become *too little*. More is not always more! When will this cultural carnival begin to lose its attraction? When will the Electronics World come of age?

Lies

Lies spawned the war in Iraq (alleged weapons of mass destruction) and lies will terminate that ill-begotten adventure (mission accomplished).

Lies have always served their nefarious purposes well! Lies and such blood cousins as deception, cheating, stealing and dishonesty are glaring evidence of life's basic contrariness.

Diminishment

With retirement, an individual's value drops abruptly. Worth then declines steadily with the passing years until eventually the individual becomes but a tolerated burden to both family and society. Death finally ends this pathetic finale and with funereal grief and sighs of relief: a blessing for both family and society.

To outlive one's significance and usefulness is a curse!

There was a time when elders were useful and respected, but that was long ago when longevity was but half of what it is today.

Our modern longevity has its price!

Some and Others

Intellectuals move and have their being in the airy virtual reality of words.

Ordinary folks tend to confine themselves to the pedestrian reality of material things.

Intellectuals might better muddy their feet a little and ordinary folks might do well to levitate a little.

The Wonder of It All

Upon occasion, when late at night, alone and enveloped by darkness and silence, I chance to reflect upon life, our planet, our solar system, the endless, timeless universe, I am left baffled in thought and over-whelmed by awe. The wonder of it all is beyond human ken and words.

The persistent attempts of science, philosophy and religion to account for this perplexing marvel have been exercises in futility. To define has only been to confine to words what is beyond our thought.

Humans can no more comprehend the wondrous universe than a speck of dust can account for the dwelling in which it chances briefly to dwell. We can do little more than bask in awe and just humbly wonder.

To Each his Own

America has long suffered from a disease called exceptionalism, a conviction that it is a nonpareil. The hallmark of this ailment is America's hallucinatory belief in a messianic mission to remake all developing countries after its own image. That its capitalistic democracy and radical individualism can't possibly be every country's cup of tea, has not deterred America in its apostolizing mission. Despite carrot and club, conversion to the American model has made little or no progress. The grandiose misadventure is continuing, notwithstanding!

"To each his own" is a maxim that America has yet to take to heart.

War is War—

Libya's "Odyssey Dawn" is yet another of America's poetically garbed designation for yet another misguided military adventure.

That which we call a war by any other name would smell as foul.

The Dance of Life

The thinking self is intent upon knowing and is anxious to avoid ignorance.

The emotional self is intent upon pleasure and is anxious to avoid pain.

The moral self is intent upon what is right and is anxious to avoid what is wrong.

The religious self is intent upon belief and is anxious to avoid hell.

To aspire to and to recoil from are the very dance of life!

Cultural Flux

*T*here was a time in the Western World, when mankind sought relief from its existential agonies by turning to religion and philosophy. For centuries, life was made more tolerable by this transcendental thinking. Eventually, however, solace and comfort gave way to doubt and disbelief, and to a renewed confrontation with the *condition humaine.* This renewed grappling with life's inexorable trials and tribulations has peaked in the relief afforded by the absorbing distraction of our Electronics Age's plethora of gadgets! What was once sought in metaphysical quest is today sought in an infatuation with electronic things novel. This new quest will ultimately be no less vain than was the old. And with that, all will be back to square one.

We will have come full circle and the cultural cycle in variation will begin all over again.

Cultures come and cultures go.

C'est la vie.

IQ

*W*hat is IQ? A measurement of total mental ability, of intelligence, mental acuity, smartness, a measurement of adroitness in the solving of problems, in the learning from experience and in reasoning.

Is IQ a constant, a designation fixed for life? Not at all! Mental ability is fluid. It can improve and can deteriorate depending upon practice. Practice does not make perfect, but it does improve skills, and if one does not use it, one will lose it. Like a knife, the mind in use can be honed and the IQ elevated. A mind in disuse, like a knife in misuse, will become dull, resulting in a lower IQ.

Is the structure of the brain a constant? No more so than the individual's IQ. Mental abilities, of which there are countless, are developed unevenly, depending upon practice. the related parts of the brain grow or shrink accordingly in their complexity.

What is constant regarding the brain? Every brain has its potentialities, and these alone are fixed, a constant determined by the individual's genes.

Potentialities, unlike abilities, are, as yet, beyond measurement.

Wondrous Madness

*M*ankind has always been far less taken with ever changing nature than given to ever changing and exploiting her. This it has done with relentless determination and with both catastrophic and astounding results. We have wasted nature by pillaging change, jeopardizing our own existence while improving it remarkably.

Mankind's mad adventure has been peculiarly paradoxical in its results. It has poisoned air, water and land, devastated wildlife and flattened forests, but its wonders in the sciences have also drastically reduced human suffering and prolonged human life beyond expectations.

In its compulsion to alter reality, mankind has left a broad wake of mad destruction and brilliant progress. Has it gone too far and is the price too high? Does all this really matter, and if so, does it matter enough for a *change*?

The Beyond and its Gods

*T*here is a beyond beyond our earthly existence—at least mankind has so insisted since time immemorial—a beyond that has teased the human imagination and has left a trail of fabulous possibilities in its wake, possibilities peopled by gods of every ilk.

The beyond and its gods have been and are likely to continue to be spiritual and moral compass, solace and comfort.

Duplicity Galore

Americans have been persuaded by their powers that be that American military interventions are a panacea for whatever ails the countries invaded, a necessary action to guarantee America's security, and an effective way to spread American democracy and liberty and to foster human rights abroad.

That the world is not so persuaded is hardly surprising!

Miracles

Beware of those who converse with God!

President George Bush brazenly informed his fellow Americans that God had chosen him to spread American democracy and liberty throughout the world.

Presidential candidate Michele Bachman would have Americans believe that God willed her to seek the presidency.

What miracle is next on the American political stage!?

Our Millennium

The prophets of the Electronics Age would have the wizards of technology bestow upon mankind what the gods have failed to do. The bestowed blessings of such solicitous geniuses as Steve Jobs and his confreres have rendered our gods dispensable. The Electronics Age has become our heaven on earth! The millennium has arrived!

Or is there a fat fly in the ointment?

Abdication of Responsibility

*M*iddle class Americans are characteristically too spent making a good living, too given to entertainment and sport and too anti-intellectual to reflect seriously on the grave social, political and economic problems besetting present-day America. Americans, as a whole are resultantly too little involved in determining what America is and what America could or should be. This does not augur well.

When the cat goes astray, the rats will have their way!

Our Lot

*M*ankind is inescapably ensnared by, and at loggerheads, with two challenging realities. The *human condition* is a given and fixed, the *social condition* is a possibility and fluid. The *existential conditions* of life are beyond any change, we can only come to terms with them. The *man-made social condition* can be changed for the better.

It is obvious that humans would do best "to accept what cannot be changed and to change what cannot be accepted."

News

*T*he explosion of readily available information of the Electronics Age is both benefit and snare. News literacy has become a must. To distinguish between fact and opinion, hearsay, propaganda, advertisement and rank lie, has become imperative. Undocumented news deserves no more than short shrift, and even documented assertions have to be carefully weighed. The wary can become well-informed and the less than alert can be thoroughly duped!

Commercial Rubbish

A cup of organic, shade-grown, fair-trade coffee must be exceptionally good, as too must be the organic cream from well-groomed, well-stabled and organically fed cows. Of course. the added sugar must be equally hallowed.

What commercial rubbish!

The Internet

*O*nly to disparage the Internet for its too much misinformation, too much questionable information and for its too much insipid gossip, is rank prejudice. The Internet's ever-growing body of significant vetted and updated information must also be duly acknowledged. This new medium will persist, and in time will shine.

The Few and the Many

*T*he growing gap between those who have and those who do not have does not augur well. It is clearly incumbent upon Washington to rectify this grossly unfair spread of America's wealth. Discreet regulation of the financial world together with a moderate increase in the income tax of the rich would do much to ameliorate the situation. Those who have little would be left with a little more and those who have more than enough would have to settle for a little less.

Tearoom Revolutionaries

*W*ere Hamlet an American of today, he would undoubtedly proclaim: Something is rotten in the state of America. And were Jesus alive in America today, he would undoubtedly side with the national

Occupy Movement and would also most certainly chase the money-changers from their Wall Street temple.

But Hamlet is fiction and Jesus is dead, and we Americans have become but tearoom revolutionaries.

Outsourcing and Automation

If outsourcing continues to grow, and if automation continues to expand, more and more workers in America will become unemployed and dispensable. This growing crucial social problem has yet to receive the political attention it deserves and must eventually get.

It is high time that the powers that be in America realize that foresight and preventative measures are by and large both less painful and less expensive than later cures.

America's Corporate Dictatorship

Corporate capitalism accrues wealth and wields plutocratic economic and political power. The general population is here only to be used for the financial world's arrogant purposes. Corporate dictatorship has become a reality in America and threatens to spread in the Western World.

How long will it be before the many dispose of this societal cancer.

Globalization

American workers cannot compete with their Chinese counterparts. The discrepancy in pay is too great. This is the price America has had to pay for globalization. While America is agonizing, China is laughing all the way to the bank.

On the other hand, American corporate capitalism has been well served by globalization. Its rapacious tentacles have spread worldwide: global exploitation.

From Detroit to Wall Street

*A*merica's economy has moved from Detroit to Wall Street. Its wealth is no longer in tangible assets but in paper profits. A house of cards has replaced factories, swelling the ranks of the wealthy and exploding the ranks of the unemployed. Nationwide rumbling of discontent is becoming ominous. A drastic change has become imperative. Will America rise to the challenge?

They Come and Go

*P*resident Th. Roosevelt's loudly proclaimed New Nationalism was nothing more than a euphemism for a budding American Imperialism. Spain, Portugal, England, France *et al* had had their imperial fling, now America prepared to exercise its military and political muscles.
America's imperial adventure seems already to have had its day!

National Medical Care

*I*nsurance corporations have made a lucrative business of health care in the U.S.A. In so doing, they have saddled America's financially solvent with the world's most costly health care policy and have left some 40 million financially-strapped Americans out in the cold. A national crisis in the making!
Such matters of national concern as America's health should clearly not be in the hands of a private health insurance industry. America's health

care should, must, and eventually will be nationalized. This change for the better is hardly revolutionary. America would simply be joining the ranks of the rest of the Western World's industrialized nations. It is high time!

America's Golden Calf

*M*oney is suffocating America's democracy. Special interest, unlimited and unidentified sums of money are literally purchasing America's politicians. Our democracy has become a plutocracy and the commonweal has become a thing of the past.

Sic transit gloria Americanae!

Privacy

*P*rivacy has always been treasured and closely guarded. In America of today, this is a thing of the past. Privacy is still treasured, but is now—thanks to the intrusive capabilities of the Electronics Age—being systematically invaded rather than guarded, and it is all being righteously done in the name of national security. The antidote may prove to be more harmful than the poison!

Cultural Metamorphosis

*O*urs has become a scientific-industrial, digitalized and thoroughly monetized world with little interest in, and no time for the human condition. This latest stage in the cultural metamorphosis of America has left a growing spiritual and moral void in its wake. How long it will be before this appalling void becomes a matter of serious concern—as it surely will—is anybody's guess.

Hopefully sooner than later!

A Circus?

America's marathon national election campaigns have become a blatant duping of the general public: a tragicomedy of empty promises, abominable lies and character assassination. Neither Barack Obama nor Mitt Romney emerge the more admirable or the more trustworthy for their orchestration of this abysmal and outrageously expensive charade. And the thinking public of America just mutters and shakes its head in disbelief!

This state of affairs must end or America will every four years become an absurd political circus. Or is that already the case?

We, the Nondescript

Scientists explicate, philosophers ruminate, professors pontificate, moralists berate, teachers regurgitate, believers fulminate and politicians bloviate. We, the remaining nondescript, are left to but masticate.

Rights and Wrongs

The rights and wrongs of yesterday are not the rights and wrongs of today, and those of today will be passé tomorrow.

Change is life's constant!

A Dour Thought

Peace is a tiresome tedious bother and war, in contrast, an adrenalin-driven exciting flurry. Little wonder that war has long been a virtual addiction in the human community. That war will ever cease to be a chronic recourse in the settling of mankind's cultural and political differences, is very unlikely.

A dour thought!

The Hucksters of our Age

*B*rilliant scientists provided the know-how for our Electronics Age, creative young entrepreneurs applied this knowledge to good advantage, and our world of novel gadgetry was born. The modest scientists have remained in the background, unacknowledged, indeed unknown. The arrogant entrepreneurs took centerstage and became both our billionaire makers and shakers and our star celebrities (Bill Gates, Steve Jobs, Larry Ellison, Mark Zuckerberg *et al*). Scientists were upstaged by hucksters! Nor was this the first time such has happened.

That Day Will Come

*I*n the U.S.A., the much of the few is appallingly more than the little of the many. And Americans are by and large too otherwise preoccupied to do anything about it. Free-market capitalism is not about to be fettered. However that day will eventually come when the many decide that change is overdue. We can but hope that the transition to something better will be more peaceful than violent.

A Plus and a Minus

*P*ain is both one of life's most common ingredients and one of life's most abhorred experiences. But this cursed discomfort is also a too little appreciated blessed warning that something is out of order and should be tended to.

Two Monoliths

*F*ree-wheeling American Capitalism has its plethora of built-in excesses, restrictive Russian Communism has its plethora of imposed excesses, and both camps have their share of virtues.

Of course, each ideology touts its own superiority, and each is only half right!

An amalgam of the best of each of these ideologies would undoubtedly be better than either!

Culture's Twilight

Shedding the constraints of civilization one by one—and this is ever more widely taking place as the twilight stage of our Christian-Judaic culture waxes—is for many an exhilarating liberating experience. Such is always the case when a culture disintegrates!

A Wonder

"Life" is an enigma, the miracle of miracles, a mystery beyond human ken. Its plethora of forms can be described but its "essence" and its "why" are beyond human thought. We can only wonder about this "wonder."

Religion and Churches

In their essence, religions are wondrous fantasy and inspirational myth, direction and goal, explanation and promise, solace and comfort. In their societal reality, religions are autocratic and oppressive, self-righteous and self-serving, arrogant and hypocritical, deceptive and bellicose.

This apparent anomaly is disturbing but should be no surprise. As an institution, religion, like all other human institutions, is but as flawed as is mankind.

To expect heaven on earth, is to expect the impossible!

Let Be What Cannot Be Changed

*L*ife has its ineluctable realities: its birth, struggle, joy, grief and its death. Not to accept these givens of the *condition humaine* is only to add to life's agonies.

But that we let be what cannot be changed, peace of mind will remain a figment of the imagination.

Compassion

*C*ompassion is one of life's most laudable virtues, and unfortunately, also one of life's many too thinly and too unevenly spread noble ingredients. Thanks to their common plight, the poor, humble and meek, are quite gregarious and tend to be decidedly more compassionate than the more individualistic and hardnosed wealthy. For the poor, compassion is solace and comfort, and for the wealthy-bound, but an impediment in their upward striving.

Feelings and Emotions

*F*eelings and emotions are spontaneous and effortless, free spirits, as it were. Thought, on the other hand, is deliberate and demands time, effort, and skill. Little wonder that the former have always been, are, and will likely remain the primary impulses in human affairs. The readier is simply more appealing than the more demanding!

Money

*I*n America, everything is monetized. Money is clearly the be-all and end-all, and this mortal disease is spreading throughout the world. A cultural antidote has yet to be found, and to quarantine is impossible. The illness will have to run its course, then self-destruct. This may take some time!

Moderation

Continuous change has become the gospel of today's world. "Change makers" are our celebrities, and novelties our passion. But constant adaption to the ever escalating change in the digital world will undoubtedly in due time become an irksome burden for the many, and novelty will pale in its attraction. And when the blush is off the bloom, enthusiasm will flag, efficiency will suffer, and declining profits will slow the pace of change. Moderation will again prove to be the guiding light of guiding lights!

A Reflection of the Mood of the Times

The Oxford dictionary has added yet another neologism to standard English: selfie, a self-taken photograph. "Me, myself and I" and "name, fame and wealth" are the digital world's banners of life. Narcissism is digital youth's credo, and is rapidly become that of the adult world. The selfie epitomizes today's adjustment to the self and to the world. This hardly bodes well!

A Meld

Capitalism in America clearly serves the few better than it serves the many. The privileged few have accumulated too much and the disadvantaged many have been left with too little. Capitalism has obviously been less interested in countering poverty than in accruing wealth. A touch of social-mindedness would do much to better the lot of the poor and to burnish capitalism's tarnished escutcheon.

America would do well to opt for a meld of capitalism and socialism before the growing unrest of its ever-widening socio-economic divide erupts in violence.

The eleventh hour is at hand!

Expediency Trumped

*E*xpediency, more than morality, occasioned Lincoln's emancipation of America's slaves.

Lincoln realized that the Civil War could be won only if the slaves in the southern states were freed, throwing the Confederate States into economic disarray.

Morality was an afterthought.

Chronic Conflict

*W*orld-wide regional conflicts have become, and are likely to remain the norm for some time to come. Good-intentioned military intervention in these civil uprisings and nation wars would leave America almost constantly engaged in warfare. Such was the case in the second half of the last century and such is threatening to be the case in the 21st century. Goodwill military intervention has only resulted in added deaths and greater destruction, in added anti-Americanism and in a colossal national debt. It is more than high time that America stop flexing its military muscle and polish its diplomatic skills.

America's Financial World

*A*merica's Stock Market has become nothing more than a National Casino. Investment has become common gambling and the gambling Casino profits at the expense of its addicted and ever hopeful clients. Brokers are not fiduciaries. They are salesmen who work on a commission basis. Commissions and not customer interest too often determine broker decision.

Our Financial World is in need of a thorough house cleaning.

Unfettered Capitalism

America's capitalism is clearly good for its capitalists, good for the wealthy and exploitative of the less fortunate many. Regulations in a world of unfettered capitalism have proven to be futile, cleverly circumvented as they are by America's resourceful financial world. But free-market capitalism will one day, not too far in the future, hit the fan and then the shit will fly!

It is high time in America for an economic system less plagued by gross financial inequality than the present system. Unfettered capitalism moderated by a touch of socialism could be a first step in the corrective direction. If nothing more, this amalgam of opposing possibilities would narrow the present untenably-wide asocial financial gap separating America's wealthy few and its wanting many, and America would be the better for it!

America and Dictators

America has long been more intent upon advantageous foreign relations than upon any laudable consistent foreign policy. Playing footsie with dictators took priority over America's vaunted spread of democracy and liberty. This must clearly change if America is to continue to enjoy international respect.

Would that . . .

Would that most Americans were taken with *the common good*.
Would that America enjoyed *a common will*.
Would that the solons of Washington were mindful of these commonalities.
Dream on Hamlet!

James Madison

"If tyranny and oppression come to this land, it will be in the guise of fighting a foreign enemy." How correct James Madison (4th president, 1809–17) was! Thanks to its serial wars, America has become a sham democracy.

America and the Middle East

America's ill-advised and ill-fated wars in Afghanistan and Iraq, and its threatened military intervention in Syria's civil war, have marred its world leadership image in the Middle East; its relationship with Pakistan has become prickly; it has fallen out of grace in Egypt and Libya; Turkey has become wary of America's presence in the Middle East; Saudi Arabia silently disapproves of its American ally; Iran would obliterate America if it could; and America's unconditional support of Israel has angered the Arab world. America's hegemony in the Middle East is clearly a thing of the past.

Freedom *ad nauseam*

America's treasured freedom was extended to the freedom of expression, and the freedom of expression, in turn, has been extended to the freedom of buying America's elections. A rapid progression from Democracy to Plutocracy! Further ill-advised extensions of freedom can only end in anarchy.

A Chameleon

America was once a Democracy. That it is no longer. It has become something of a chameleon. Some would term it an Aristocracy of the Wealthy, for others it is now a Plutocracy, and for yet others a Corporatocracy. The playful would have it be a Dollarocracy or a Digitalocracy. One thing is certain: America is not what it used to be, and change has not been for the better.

Unfettered Capitalism

*U*nfettered capitalism has left America torn by divides, tensions and inequalities. Unless America's capitalism becomes more conscious of the common good and begins to act accordingly, it will eventually be its own undoing. There still is time for self-correction.
Will wise heads prevail?

America's Stewardship

*P*olitics, finance and technology are the three major forces that characterize and drive America. The political world is in turmoil, the financial world is rapacious and the technical world is starry-eyed. Given this wanting stewardship, America's future is unlikely to warm the cockles of many hearts.

Ever More

A merica's is a growth economy. For the economy to ever grow, the many are ever persuaded to consume ever more. While the many spend themselves into ever more debt and poverty, the few and their corporations add ever more to their vast accumulation of wealth.

A Metamorphosis

America has become a technologized, dollarized and polarized plutocracy, characterized by materialism, consumerism, hedonism, radical individualism, unfettered capitalism, imperialism and militarism, a brew that does not bode well.

The democracy, liberty and equality espoused by America's founding fathers have flown the coop and there is little promise that they will soon, if ever, return.

A pity!

The Tin Lizzie, its Heirs, and Consequences

Our deadly motorized tin cans on four rubberized wheels, and their ubiquitous web of ugly concrete roads, have polluted earth's atmosphere and devastated its land. What a price for our ingenious convenience!

It's high time that this common fascination be superannuated. Surely there are better and less costly ways to get from here to there and back again!

Life

Life is inert matter become miraculously alive. It is intent solely upon remaining alive and propagating. Such compelling needs and appetites as thirst, hunger and sexual drive serve these two purposes well. For life, there is no intrinsic good or evil, no heaven or earth, there is but an "is" or "is not."

C'est la vie!

Political Transition

A country torn by civil strife is best served by an enlightened dicta-torship. And only after peace and the rule of law have been re-estab-lished, should an enlightened dictatorship give way to a representative democracy. This transition demands political acumen, time and patience.

Agricultural Transition

*F*arming, once a family commitment, has become a production-line industry. What was small, personal and often inefficient, has become very large, quite impersonal, highly efficient and very productive. Much, humanly treasured, was lost, but more, nutritionally necessary, was found!

Our Reality

"*W*ere" implies we are no more, "is" implies we are, and "will be" implies that we are not yet. As such, we are a visible sequence.
Pondered philosophically, this sequence melds, becoming a timeless oneness. the present moment incorporates all that was and all that will be. All is oneness and timelessness.
Appearance tells one story, and mystical reflection tells another!

Last Questions

*W*hat did you make of yourself?
What did you do for society?
What will you bequeath posterity?
Haunting questions!

Wants and Rights

*I*n America, of late, wants have commonly become needs, and these needs are commonly becoming legislated rights. This loosening of America's cultural fabric is symptomatic of the twilight of the Western World's Judeo-Christian culture. Much that was wrong has become right, and ever more that was right is becoming wrong. Cultures come and cultures go!

Buddha

*B*uddha turned his back upon mankind's stressful lot to embrace a stressless nothingness. Better death than life! So much for Buddha's Eastern Wisdom!

The Female and the Male

*T*he female and her children are a world of their own. The male is but a necessary adjunct. The male is a means, an indispensable fringe factor in procreation and in the sustenance of mother and child. The female, in contrast, is the very seed of life, life incarnate, reality's mother, our *sine qua non*.

Artificial Intelligence

*W*hat has popularly been termed artificial intelligence might more correctly be termed electronic skill. The fear that artificial intelligence will in time surpass human intelligence is a stretch of the imagination. Artificial intelligence, better electronic skill, will continue to assist and not replace human intelligence.

Cultural Turmoil

*T*he Judeo-Christian culture of our democracy-minded Western World has well nigh run its troubled course and will, in due time, like the cultures of antiquity, become quaint history.

The Islamic culture of the Middle East's autocratic Arab World, like our Judeo-Christian culture, is rent and spent, wallowing in its throes of death.

In both instances, the dying old will give way to a birthing new. the Greek and Roman worlds did not spring up overnight, nor will the new Western and Middle East Worlds. The trying transition from old to new is likely to drag on for decades, and the beliefs and values of the resultant new cultures have yet to begin to crystallize. *They will*, and the whole world, at least for a time, will be the better for it.

An Ominous Trend

*I*ndividually and nationally, empathy and understanding, goodwill and benevolence, and tolerance and pacifism, are globally steadily waning, and antipathy and ignorance, animosity and malice, and acrimony and belligerence are waxing just as globally and just as continuously. Given the global sweep and impetus of this ominous trend, the world is likely to be left culturally devastated before it begins to change for the better.

Cultural Mechanics

*A*merica's materialism, consumerism, capitalism and technology have dehumanized America's culture. Ours has become a thing-minded culture, and we have become thing-obsessed humans. Humans can change cultures for the worse, and these cultures, in turn, will change humans for the worse. Fortunately, the opposite also takes place!

Essayistic Ventures and Topical Asides

America's Make-Believe Reality

Our cowboys of yore had their horses and cows.
Our hero mobsters of the early 20th century had their slick cars and gangs.
And our current electronic techies have their world of digital gadgetry and their myriad millions.
America's story has chapters that are stranger than fiction!

Islam

Many of Islam's cultural dams have recently collapsed and are spilling a torrent of confusion, bewilderment and madness, and are leaving behind a swath of death and destruction. Some cultures collapse in final bouts of debauchery, hilarity and licentiousness; other past cultures have done what Islam is doing. Two forms of cultural madness!

Robots

Robots and artificial intelligence have become realities that promise to become ever more sophisticated. That there will be astounding social and personal consequences, both positive and negative, is inevitable. Immediately, robots promise to augment the work force, and eventually they may replace humans. Time will tell whether society or the individual will emerge the better for this critical turn in human history.

A Hoax

It was not America's loudly proclaimed security-mindedness or its ardently argued spread of democracy that determined its aggressive foreign policy. All this was but a brazen calculated public relations ploy.

It was America's long-time empire-mindedness and not self-defence and/or propagation of democracy that motivated its bellicose foreign policy. America, the world's dominant political, economic and military power, was, and is still, simply guaranteeing its pre-eminence by checkmating all aspiring world powers both politically and militarily. Hegemonies are time-bound and America's will be no exception. Time is running out!

A Lament

Socially, America is deeply troubled.
Politically, it is an alarming disarray.
And financially, it is seriously divided.
Drastic changes for the better are long overdue!

ABOUT THE AUTHOR

Joseph Mileck was born in Sanktmartin, Roumania in 1922, immigrated to Canada in 1926 and again in 1931. He has a B.A. Degree from McMaster University, Hamilton, Ontario (1945), and a PhD. from Harvard University (1950). Joseph was a member of the German Department of the University of California, Berkeley from 1950 to 1991. He has published five books and numerous articles, dealing with such German authors as Franz Kafka, Thomas Mann and Hermann Hesse. He has also edited two cultural-historical books about Sanktmartin, a typical German community in Roumania, and has published a book-length study of that community's dialect. To these scholarly works, published from 1951 to 2003, Joseph has added four collections of his own poetry and epigrams: *A Trail of Poetic Reflection*. Berkeley, California: Beatitude Press, 2008, 114 pp.; *A Medley of Piquant Poetry and Edgy Epigrams*. Berkeley, California: Beatitude Press, 2010, 126 pp.; *More Salt and Pepper. Poems and Epigrams*. Berkeley, California: Beatitude Press, 2012, 173 pp.; and *Pensive Pauses. Epigrams and Poems*. Berkeley, California: Pensive Oasis Press, 2016, 226 pp.

To his many literary bibliographical, linguistic, and socio-political books, Mileck added a critical appraisal of the United States: *America. An Empire in Disarray*. Berkeley, California, Beatitude Press, 2013, 172 pp.